Power to Tread

Deliverance and Exorcism Guidelines for Christians

Mitsi Burton

Power to Tread, by Mitsi Burton

ISBN # 0-89228-159-6

Impact Christian Books
332 Leffingwell Ave.,
Kirkwood, MO 63122
314-822-3309
www.impactchristianbooks.com

Cover Design: *Ideations*

Printed in the United States of America

Index

Part 1: The Basics

Part 2 : Legal Rights of Demons

Part 3 : The Practice of Deliverance

Part 1

The Basics

But this is people robbed and spoiled; they are all of them snared in holes, and they are hid in prison houses: they are for a prey, and none delivereth; for a spoil, and none saith, Restore.
Isaiah 42: 22

Behold, I give you
power to tread
on serpents and scorpions
and over all of the power of the enemy
and nothing shall
by any means
hurt you.

Luke 10:19

Christians Can And Do Have Demons

This is the first question that Christians ask deliverance ministers. Although there are good teachings that say otherwise, the facts prove that demons can indeed dwell in Christians. This is demonstrated continually in the practice of the deliverance ministry. I have heard Christians state that demons are oppressing us from the outside, hanging around us or sitting on our shoulders (wishful thinking), but the fact of the matter is that they are doing their dirty work from inside us. If they were not inside, we would not have to cast them "out."

A lot of Christians get very touchy about this subject, and I do not blame them. I don't want those things inside of me, either. In fact, I had such strong feelings about it, that I wanted to make sure that I got rid of them, if I had them. Maybe I did not know enough "theology" at the time, but I was not terribly sure that I did **not** have them. I found out I **did** have demons! I was not possessed, but plenty of demons came out of me in my first deliverance session.

Some of you might be thinking, "Well, maybe she did bad things." Believe me, I had committed my average sins before I was a born-again Christian. I had not killed anybody; I had not held up a bank; I had not done drugs or witchcraft, etc. Just the average little sins that in the eyes of the Father might be worse. *"As it is written, there is none righteous, no, not one,"* ***Romans 3:10***.

The Way We Have Been Created

1 Thessalonians 5:23
And the very God of peace sanctify you wholly; and I pray God your whole spirit and soul and body be preserved blameless unto the coming of our Lord Jesus Christ.

Hebrews 4:12
For the Word of God is quick, and powerful, and sharper than any twoedged sword, piercing even to the dividing asunder of soul and spirit, and of the joints and marrow, and is a discerner of the thoughts and intents of the heart.

The first Scripture tells us that we were created by God as a body that contains a soul and a spirit. The second Scripture tells us that the soul and spirit are separated and made distinct by the Word of God.

Most psychologists and scientists are of the opinion that soul and spirit are the same thing. In fact, some pastors are of this opinion even when the Bible states many times that there is a soul and a spirit.

Luke 1:46-47
And Mary said, My soul doth magnify the Lord, And my spirit hath rejoiced in God my Saviour.

Mary, the mother of Jesus, knew she had a soul and a spirit. In many of the Psalms, David states that he has a soul and a spirit, except that in the Old Testament, the word used for "spirit" is "heart."

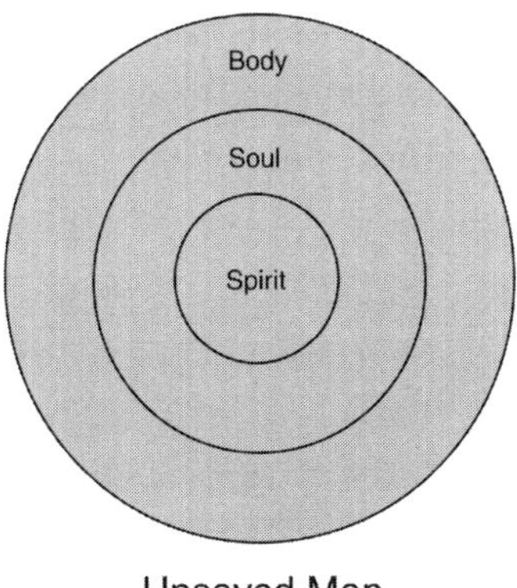

Unsaved Man

When we become born-again Christians, our spirit is cleansed. There is a noticeable change in most born-again people. Our tastes change. Our way of looking at things change. I personally even perceived daylight to be brighter. This is because any unclean spirits residing in the human spirit leave as the Holy Spirit enters the human spirit. After this happens, demons can no longer enter the human spirit, not only because of the indwelling presence of the Holy Spirit, but also because the human spirit is sealed by the Holy Spirit. There is a spiritual seal in the human spirit that is branded with the name of Jesus.

When I say there is a seal on your spirit, I mean if you

had spiritual eyes, you could see it. For many centuries, kings wore a signet ring and used it to imprint their seal on their official documents. This is how our spiritual seal is, and our king is Jesus. One of the tactics you can use to weaken demons is to command them to look at the person's spirit and tell you what they see. They will report that they see a seal with the name "Jesus" imprinted on it. Demons hate to look at it, because they know they are trespassing.

2 Corinthians 1:21-22
Now he which stablisheth us with you in Christ, and hath anointed us, is God; Who hath also sealed us, and given the earnest of the Spirit in our hearts.

Remember, "our hearts" means "our spirits."

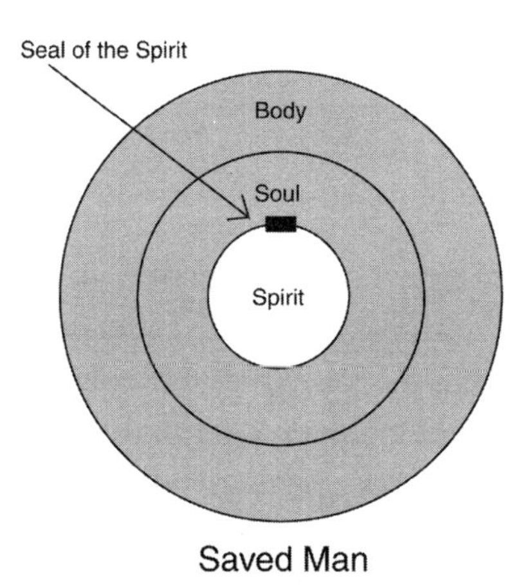

Saved Man

Thus, a Christian cannot be possessed. However, our soul and body are still under the influence of demons. Through deliverance we can get rid of those demons. This should be our goal.

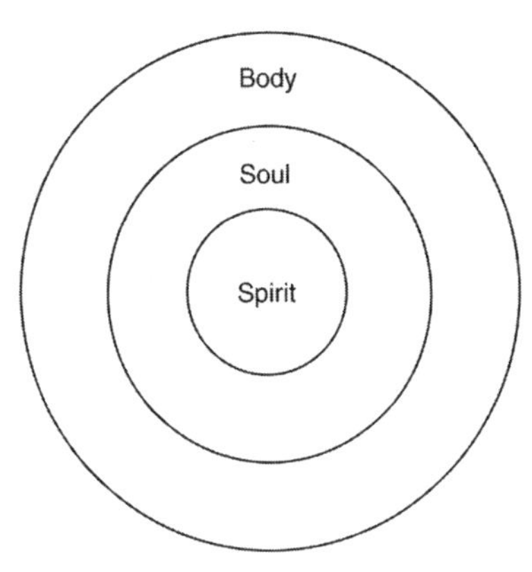

The Christian Man's Goal

A man that has not made Jesus Christ his Lord and Savior does not have the protective seal in his human spirit. If this man engages in abominable living, his spirit is at risk of being controlled by demons, thus he becomes possessed.

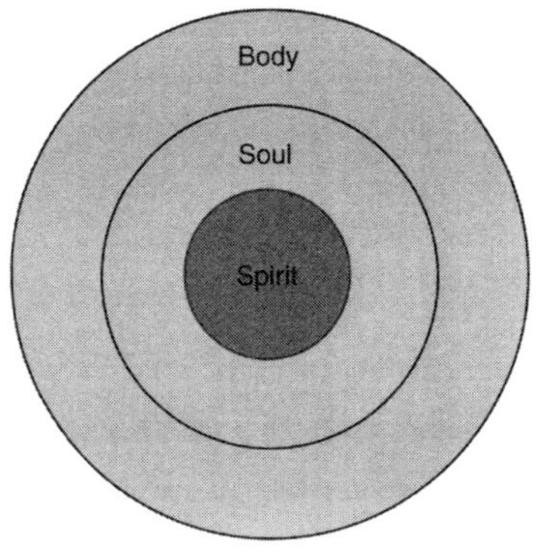

Possessed Man

What Demons do in the Body and Soul of a Christian.

In the body, the demons can cause sickness and infirmities, imbalances, deformities, pains, dysfunctions and abnormalities.

The soul is composed of the mind, the emotions and the will. Our personality is our soul. When a person seems to have more than one personality, it is the result of demons working in the soul. Sometimes a person refers to a bad characteristic of their personality saying, "I can't control it. This is the way I am." This shows the work that demons do in the soul, changing the person's personality for the worse, and at the same time convincing the person that what they are experiencing is merely their own personality.

Mind: In the mind, the demons attack with confusion, forgetfulness, retardation, learning disabilities, fantasies, visions, paranoia, etc.

Emotions: The emotions are attacked with jealousy, rejection, shyness, fear, inferiority, lust, depression, resentment, hate, etc.

Will: When the will is attacked, the person can't break bad habits. The demons provoke inertia. The person tries to stop smoking, drinking, gambling, overeating, etc. and does not succeed.

Of course, it is not as simple as stated above. The devil will attack with the same purpose in more than one area, i.e. the mind and the will, or the emotions, the will and the body, etc.

The Bible Tells Us that Believers Can Have Demons

Please study the following Scriptures:

Matthew 15:21-28

Then Jesus went thence, and departed into the coasts of Tyre and Sidon. And, behold, a woman of Canaan came out of the same coasts, and cried unto him, saying, Have mercy on me, O Lord, thou Son of David; my daughter is grievously vexed with a devil. But he answered her not a word. And his disciples came and besought him, saying, Send her away; for she crieth after us. But he answered and said, I am not sent but unto the lost sheep of the house of Israel. Then came she and worshipped him, saying, Lord, help me. But he answered and said, It is not meet to take ***the children's bread****, and to cast it to dogs. And she said, Truth, Lord: yet the dogs eat of the crumbs which fall from their masters' table. Then Jesus answered and said unto her, O woman, great is thy faith: be it unto thee even as thou wilt. And her daughter was made whole from that very hour.*

Mark 7:24-30

And from thence he arose, and went into the borders of Tyre and Sidon, and entered into an house, and would have no man know it: but he could not be hid. For a certain woman, whose young daughter had an unclean spirit, heard of him, and came and fell at his feet: The woman was a Greek, a Syrophenician by nation; and she besought him that he would cast forth the devil out of her daughter. But Jesus said unto her, Let the children first be filled: for it is not meet to take ***the children's bread****, and to cast it unto the dogs. And she answered and said unto him, Yes, Lord: yet the dogs under the table eat of the children's crumbs. And he said unto her, For this saying go thy way; the devil is gone out of thy daughter. And when she was come to her house, she found the devil gone out, and her daughter laid upon the bed.*

After studying these Scriptures, answer the following questions:

1. Was the woman from the house of Israel?__________

2. Did she worship the God of Israel?_______________

3. What was the problem with her daughter?__________

4. What did the woman want Jesus to do for her daughter?______________________________

5. How did Jesus react to her request? ______________________________________

6. When He did speak, what did He say? ______________________________________

7. What did He answer to her request? ____________ ______________________________________

8. What did Jesus call the deliverance she was asking for?________________________________

9. Who are the "children" today?_________________ ______________________________________

The woman was not Jewish. She was pagan or gentile, and she was requesting something that was reserved only for believers. Jesus would not even answer her at first. Then He said that He had come only to the house of Israel, not to unbelievers (or pagans, who were called "dogs" by the Jews). Following this, He said that what she wanted, deliverance, was "the children's bread," meaning that deliverance was not for unbelievers.

There were several qualities in this woman that made Jesus give her what she asked. First, she came asking Him and not her pagan gods. Maybe those gods had already demonstrated to her that they were useless. Another quality was her persistence. The disciples had already rejected her, but she would not go away. That took faith. She was humble and not offended when He said, "This is not for you, lady, this is only for us, a different class of people." What would the average person say today? "You are calling me names, I'll sue you. I have a right to get what the others are getting. You are discriminating against me."

This woman accepted her condition of being "under the table, eating the crumbs." There was a lot of humility in her. And finally, her faith. She really believed in Jesus. She persisted, knowing that He could give her what she needed. That qualified her as a believer! So she received deliverance, *the children's bread*, for her daughter. Jesus lifted her to eat at the table.

These Scriptures show that Jesus considered (and still considers) deliverance to belong to believers and not to unbelievers.

Who Are The Children?

In the previous study, we learned that Jesus called deliverance "the children's bread." To what children was Jesus referring? In several Scriptures we can see that the Lord made a distinction among the Jews, calling some of them "children of Abraham" and others "descendants" or "seed" of Abraham. The following study is based on a teaching by Norman Parish.

Luke 13:10-16

And he was teaching in one of the synagogues on the sabbath. And, behold, there was a woman which had a spirit of infirmity eighteen years, and was bowed together, and could in no wise lift up herself. And when Jesus saw her, he called her to him, and said unto her, Woman, thou art loosed from thine infirmity. And he laid his hands on her: and immediately she was made straight, and glorified God. And the ruler of the synagogue answered with indignation, because that Jesus had healed on the sabbath day, and said unto the people, There are six days in which men ought to work: in them therefore come and be healed, and not on the sabbath day. The Lord then answered him, and said, Thou hypocrite, doth not each one of you on the sabbath loose his ox or his ass from the stall, and lead him away to watering? And ought not this woman, being a ***daughter of Abraham****, whom Satan hath bound, lo, these eighteen years, be loosed from this bond on the sabbath day?*

Here is a woman worshiping the God of Israel in the synagogue. She had a demon of infirmity. Jesus called her "a daughter of Abraham." When delivered, she glorified God. In the same sentence that Jesus said the woman was a daughter of Abraham, He also said that Satan had her bound for 18 years. In this Scripture, Jesus himself said that she was a child of God, and that she had a demon at the same time. With this evidence, how can people say that Christians can't have demons?

John 8:37-41

I know that ye are Abraham's seed; but ye seek to kill me, because my word hath no place in you. I speak that which I have seen with my Father: and ye do that which ye have seen with your father. They answered and said unto him, Abraham is our father. Jesus saith unto them, If ye were Abraham's children, ye would do the works of Abraham. But now ye seek to kill me, a man that hath told you the truth, which I have heard of God: this did not Abraham. You do the deeds of your father.

The Jews of the temple wanted to kill Jesus. He calls them Abraham's seed, not Abraham's children. In fact, He implied that their father was Satan.

Luke 3:8
Bring forth therefore fruits worthy of repentance, and begin not to say within yourselves, We have Abraham to our father: for I say unto you, That God is able of these stones to raise up children unto Abraham.

In this Scripture, John the Baptist says that it is not necessary to be a seed or descendant of Abraham to be a child of Abraham. The Jews are seed of Abraham through the flesh, but both Jews and Gentiles can be children of Abraham through the Spirit, that is, being born of the Spirit of God.

Galatians 3:7
Know ye therefore that they which are of faith, the same are the children of Abraham.

If you are a born-again Christian, you are "of faith," and you are a child of Abraham. In Jesus' time, the Jews who believed were children of Abraham. Going back to the woman in the synagogue (Luke 13:10), Jesus referred to her as a daughter of Abraham and immediately added that she had been bound by Satan for 18 years. Born-again Christians are also children of Abraham and can also be bound by Satan. The difference now is that Jesus has given us power to cast the demons out, which the believing Jews did not have yet.

Those who say that Christians cannot have demons are

doing Satan a favor. Whoever teaches this lie is responsible for Christians not seeking and receiving deliverance. This is the reason for problems in the churches, from the pastor to the youngest member. Churches have split and broken up because of jealousy, gossip, adultery, greed, envy, and all kinds of demonic work. Pastors and evangelists have fallen into the hands of demons of lust, adultery and greed. When a pastor does not admit that Christians can have demons (and much less himself), Satan has an easy time destroying the church and the pastor. Jesus left us a command to cast out demons, but it is not being obeyed. Remember that Jesus is coming for a church without spot or wrinkle!

Sure, the flesh has a part in the problems, but for those who are really trying to please God and put the flesh down, it is very hard to do while there are demons who incite the flesh.

Deliverance Is Not For The Lost

Deliverance is only for Christians. It is the children's bread. If we minister deliverance to a person who is not saved, and the person does not accept Jesus as his/her Lord, that person might end up worse than before. This lost person does not have the seal of the Spirit in his/her spirit. You have to be careful whether or not to minister (better ask the Lord), because someone who is used to going to a witch or a spiritualist to have their problems solved might come to you for ministry just to get rid of a pain or something else that torments him/her.

They might tell you that they are Christians, and they might receive deliverance. But they are not committed to live for Christ. See what happens then:

Matthew 12:43-45
When the unclean spirit is gone out of a man, he walketh through dry places, seeking rest, and findeth none. Then he saith, I will return into my house from whence I came out; and when he is come, he findeth it empty, swept, and garnished. Then goeth he, and taketh with himself seven other spirits more wicked than himself, and they enter in and dwell there: and the last state of that man is worse than the first. Even so shall it be also unto this wicked generation.

Jesus said that when the "house" is empty, the demon that was cast out comes back with seven worse. The "house" is the spirit of the man, and the Holy Spirit is not there, so the "house" is empty.

What the Lord was saying is that not only did the man not have the Holy Spirit in him, but he was also ready to receive more and worse demons, because of disobedience to God. If you read all of Leviticus chapter 26, you will find that the Lord is warning us that He punishes disobedience, and if we are still disobedient, He will punish us seven times worse. See Chapter 14, *How To Minister Deliverance*, for a more detailed explanation of Matthew 12:43-45.

This is why we should not minister deliverance to people who are not born-again Christians. Deliverance is the children's bread, only for Christians. The only way to safely minister deliverance to someone who is lost, is as follows:

a) If the Lord tells you to go ahead with the deliverance, and

b) If you are sure that what is holding the person back from asking Jesus to be his/her Lord is a demon that needs to be cast out.

2

Exorcism and deliverance have the same goal: to cast out demons. The practice of exorcism is very old. The practice of deliverance is only 2005 years old at this writing. Why? Because the Lord Jesus Christ brought us deliverance.

Exorcism

No one can tell when men started performing exorcisms, but they have been recorded in the ancient histories of Babylon and Egypt. Exorcisms are related to magic and are practiced today by pagan native religions or witchcraft of several different cultures. They are performed through rituals using objects believed to draw the demons out.

In Mexico, Curanderos (medicine men) use a fresh egg that is rubbed on the patient's body. After the ritual is finished, the egg is cracked open by the Curandero and the contents are shown. A Mexican woman I know who had the ritual performed on her told me that her egg contained a fat worm. Another story I heard from my daughter who had a Mexican friend whom she was telling about deliverance included a tomato that had the contents of a little demonic head with horns. Others have reported different things, none pretty. In Cuba, the Santeria priests perform a "limpia" (cleansing) using cigar smoke, which they blow upon the patient, and branches taken from a basil plant, which they use to sweep over the patient's body, like a broom.

Babylonians made clay dolls into which demons were transferred through magic. Then, they would destroy the dolls believing the demons would be destroyed.

King Solomon used to perform exorcisms. The Jewish historian Josephus in the book, *Complete Works* (Kregel Publications), relates the following:

"God also enabled him to learn that skill which expels demons, which is a science useful and sanative to men. He composed such incantations also by which distempers are alleviated. And he left behind him the manner of using exorcisms, by which they drive away demons, so that they never return, and this method of cure is of a great force unto this day...."

Then, Josephus relates how a man, following the instructions that Solomon left, performed an exorcism: "He put a ring that had a root of one of those sorts mentioned by Solomon to the nostrils of the demoniac, after which he drew out the demon through the nostrils; and when the man fell down, immediately he abjured him to return into him no more, making still mention of Solomon, and reciting the incantations which he had composed...."

In a footnote the book's editor mentions that Solomon learned this from his pagan wives and not from God, and I agree with him.

In the Bible, you can't find the word "exorcism." The only place you find the word "exorcists" is in the following Scripture:

Acts 19:13-16

Then certain of the vagabond Jews, exorcists, took upon them to call over them which had evil spirits the name of the Lord Jesus, saying, We adjure you by Jesus whom Paul preacheth. And there were seven sons of one Sceva, a Jew, and chief of the priests, which did so. And the evil spirit answered and said, Jesus I know, and Paul I know; but who are ye? And the man in whom the evil spirit was leaped on them, and overcame them, and prevailed against them, so that they fled out of that house naked and wounded.

In these Scriptures, these men are called vagabond exorcists. Exorcism was popular in Israel and the surrounding countries at the time of Jesus and even before His time. Exorcists probably made a living at it, and they traveled offering their services. The people of the time were used to seeing exorcisms and also easily recognized the need for an exorcism (unlike today). These particular exorcists traveled and performed exorcisms in homes. The seven were brothers, sons of the chief priest, so they would have been priests themselves. They might have been performing exorcisms for some time but not believing that Jesus was the son of God. However, at some point they realized that it was much easier to cast out demons in the name of Jesus, so they tried it. The demon knew they did not have that power or permission from the Lord, so the demon attacked, hurt, stripped and humiliated them.

Acts 19:17

And this was known to all the Jews and Greeks also dwelling at Ephesus; and fear fell on them all, and the name of the Lord Jesus was magnified.

The people who knew about this debacle also knew how Paul had cast out demons. They knew there was a big difference in the results, and they realized that the power of God was with Paul. The fear of God fell on them, and they confessed and repented of their deeds. This is the difference between exorcism and deliverance.

Acts 19:18-19

And many that believed came, and confessed, and shewed their deeds. Many of them also which used curious arts brought their books together, and burned them before all men: and they counted the price of them, and found it fifty thousand pieces of silver.

That was true repentance!

Today, several Christian denominations perform exorcisms. The Catholic Church performs them only on the possessed. I recommend you read *Hostage to the Devil* by Malachi Martin (Harper San Francisco, Harper Collins Publishers) to know how Catholic exorcisms are performed. According to the book, Catholic priests believe they must suffer at the hands of the demons. They are sure that, once they get into exorcism, they do not have long to live. During the exorcism, they must be prepared for levitation and flying objects, so they must remove furniture and lock all doors and windows.

Several years ago, I saw the movie, *The Exorcist*. Years later, the Lord called me to the deliverance ministry. Remembering the movie, I thought, based on my own experience, that it was a Hollywood exaggeration, since I never saw anything nearly like what the movie showed when I ministered. I kept thinking that it was all fantasy and drama, until I read *Hostage to the Devil.* Then, I realized that the movie was mild compared to the book.

Deliverance

Deliverance emerged with the Lord Jesus Christ. As you read the Gospels, you realize that Jesus did not use any herbs, rings, eggs, or anything else other than His authority over the demons. He showed a better way to cast out demons through the power of God, and He gave His followers the same power. But remember, only His true followers are able to receive this power, and the demons can tell whether or not you have the power of God in you or not.

Luke 10:19
Behold, I give unto you power to tread on serpents and scorpions, and over all the power of the enemy: and nothing shall by any means hurt you.

Evangelicals call the casting out of demons deliverance, but casting out or driving demons out of inanimate objects or buildings is called exorcism.

How to Exorcize Your Home

I have been called many times by mothers whose children wake up frightened in the middle of the night and want to sleep with their parents. Some children say that there are "monsters" in their bedroom. Even college-age kids have felt afraid as they sense a presence in the room. In one particular case, the "presence" would come out of an antique wardrobe. I anointed the houses and commanded the demons to leave and not return, and the problem was solved.

The children, who did not know what I had done, slept soundly and felt a difference in their rooms. Some of them had toys that were demonic in appearance, such as Darth Vader toys or monster-looking toys, and those were destroyed.

Most people believe they have to anoint doors and windows to expel demons from a house, and I wonder where this teaching came from. I can see the Passover blood anointing of the door as a basis for it, but it does not make any sense for driving demons out of your house. The blood on the doors Passover night in Egypt was a signal to the angel of death not to enter that home. Spirits can walk through walls, but even if they couldn't, anointing the windows and doors would *preven*t them from coming out that way.

Here is how to do it. Pour a small amount of fresh olive oil into a little cup. Pray to the Lord that He will anoint or empower the oil for driving demons out of your house and property. Do not use oil with spices, and absolutely **do not** use the formula in the Old Testament to create anointing oil. In these Scriptures, there is a curse that comes upon those who use the compounded oil for anything other than anointing priests. Your prayer to the Lord will be enough for the oil to become anointing oil for the purpose you desire.

Then, go to the <u>dark places</u> of the house and anoint - just a touch of your finger dipped in the oil - and command the demons that are there to leave in Jesus' name and never to return.

You are probably asking yourself, "What are the dark places?" Nothing mystical or religious about it. The dark places are the places where light does not reach. Under beds, inside closets, behind furniture, inside drawers and cabinet doors, the attic, etc.

You can exorcize furniture or other objects that you suspect may have demons in the same way, unless the objects are abominations such as idols (little buddhas, animal statues, etc.), and those must be destroyed. More will be explained about this later.

The Antique Chairs

Years ago, I bought a set of antique Chippendale-style chairs for my dining room from an antique store. The owner of the antique shop told me the chairs came from a convent in Galveston. After I became a born-again believer, I started noticing that whenever I was reading my Bible, I could hear the chairs "snap, crackle and pop". I kept telling myself that the humidity and temperature changes in Houston would swell up and dry out the wood, pulling on the joints and causing the noises. Reasonable, right? One day, as I was reading my Bible, I was distracted again by the noises. The Holy Spirit suddenly told me, "The chairs have demons." Immediately, I anointed them one by one with oil and commanded all the demons to leave. The chairs never made another noise.

Exorcizing Your Pets

The following is an experience my daughter had in exercising her newfound faith in deliverance:

About six months after Miss Kitty died, one Saturday, I decided to adopt another female kitten from the SPCA, and I found one I liked. The SPCA wouldn't let her leave until she was spayed, so I had to pick her up on Monday. She was only about nine weeks old. I was concerned.

I returned and found a frightened little kitten with runny eyes. The caretaker told me that this upper-respiratory infection was common among the cats which were spayed, and she gave me some medicine. I was mildly horrified to be starting off again from the SPCA with a sick kitten.

When I brought her home, she perked up and seemed to be quite happy with her new environment, inspecting everything. But I noticed she wouldn't eat. Dad and Mom took her to the vet the next day. The doctor gave her a shot to bring down her fever and new medicine. They sent home a porridge for me to force feed her through a syringe. The problem with that was that she couldn't breathe as it was, and then feeding her caused her to choke. I had no experience with this and I fed her too much at one time. I thought she was going to die.

Her breathing began to worsen, and she became listless. I brought her back to the vet, and she spent two full days there with the nurses trying to figure out how to get her to breathe and eat, and re-hydrating her. Her medicine changed again in an effort to fight off an infection or virus or both. Poor thing had just been spayed at nine weeks, had worms, and had this breathing problem to boot. Not eating just worsened her body[1]s ability to fight the infection. She had also stopped drinking, which made me worry about her little kidneys.

The vet tried a humidifier, which he claimed helped her breathe. I ran to the store that night to buy one. I remembered we had a vaporizer when I was a child. As I was standing in front of the display of humidifiers and vaporizers, my gut (I think the Holy Spirit) was telling me to buy a vaporizer, but I kept hearing the doctor tell me "humidifier," so I bought one.

When I plugged it in, it emitted cold air, which surprised me. I kept thinking of the steam that the vaporizer emitted. I put Gracie in the bathroom on a heating pad with the humidifier and closed the door for the night. I was horrified in the morning to find that the bathroom was cold, and she started crying at me as if she were cold too.

That was Saturday morning. I went into a panic because she was struggling so much with breathing. I ran back to the store and got a vaporizer, came home, plugged it in and turned on a hot shower to really steam up the bathroom. I did that all day long and it helped.

Three times that day, Gracie stopped breathing. She was actually starting to feel better, it seemed, so she started bathing herself, and as she did, it seemed to stop up her nose. The first time it happened, she started going into a convulsion and I couldn't figure out what was going on. I just shook her a little and she would eventually come out of it. The second time I noticed she was bathing and had her head way down, and when she brought it back up, that's when she started convulsing. I was on the phone with a friend, and she was the one who said that maybe she had stopped breathing. I remembered the first time she did this, her head was down too. I thought, that must be what it is—all her mucous is running to her nose and plugging it up, and she can't get any air in her lungs.

The rest of the day, whenever she'd start bathing, I'd try to discourage it. She went into a convulsion one more time, but I shook her up and in about a minute she came out of it.

In the midst of all these physical manifestations of her illness and the impending sense of doom I felt for this little kitten that I had fallen in love with, I started thinking about why this was happening. Like most people who become seriously ill, "why me?" seems to plague the mind. I began to put into practice all the spiritual warfare that my mother had taught me, as well as some things I had learned from Andrew Wommack, a TV minister whom I follow regularly.

As I started meditating on all the issues and problems, the enemy kept tormenting me with thoughts that the cat was going to die. So, one of my first lines of reasoning through this was, "Why would God create an animal or a baby (or technically, create procreation), just so it could die?" I could hear the vet now: "Well, we don't know why these things happen, but some kittens and puppies just die." I wasn't willing to accept that. Then, I heard in my head, "It was just God's will," like a lot of good, but uneducated, church-going people say. I started rebuking these thoughts. I just couldn't accept that it was God's will, and I just knew that it wasn't. It just didn't make sense. I started believing that this was an attack of Satan and forming my plan of counter-attack. I started thinking that perhaps because I am now a PK (preacher's kid), he really has it out for me, but he'll never win because "the weapons of our warfare are not carnal but mighty through God to the pulling down of strongholds" (II Corinthians 10:3-5).

Tuesday night of that week (the day after I picked Gracie up) was my first night for real spiritual warfare. I put the kitty to bed and I got angry at Satan. I started yelling at him and shaking my fist, pacing in my home. I remembered Andrew Wommack's story of how he did the same thing when he was in deep poverty and couldn't pay his bills. When he unleashed his fury on Satan, amazing resolutions to his problems began to happen (Matthew 11:12).

I started first with thanking the Lord for the gift he had given me of Gracie, and that in His Word, He wants us to take care of His animals, that He knows when a sparrow falls to the ground (Matthew 10:29), and I wanted to take care of Gracie. I told him that if demons would ask Jesus to enter a flock of pigs (Matthew 8:32), then I felt that maybe there was some demonically-related illness going on with Gracie. I thanked the Lord for dying on the cross and rising from His grave to give us the power to tread on serpents,

(Luke 10:19) and this was one serpent I was definitely going to tread on. I told Him I knew it was not His will that she die. I kept repeating that and believing that. I told Him I knew that He gives good gifts to His children (Matthew 7:11, Luke 11:12).

I started telling Satan he was a liar, a thief and a destroyer (John 10:10). He had destroyed two marriages in my life, kept me from having children, took my beloved cat from me earlier in the year, and on and on. I told him he wasn't going to steal anything else, and that included Gracie. I just ranted and raved at him and quoted Scripture, like Proverbs 6:31, where a caught thief has to restore sevenfold. I told Satan to get out of her and get out of my house. When I got through with him, I started asking the Lord for healing for Gracie.

Wednesday night I couldn't sleep from worry. Demons of fear and anxiety kept waking me up. I had to keep rebuking them through the night.

Thursday night, I took a walk in my neighborhood and started praying in English and tongues. I kept meditating on the cat's illness and I started to think about curses that may be causing her to be so sick (Proverbs 6:2). I started breaking everything that came to my mind: spoken words from my father, the vet and his staff, like, "I don't think she's going to make it," or "She's probably going to die," etc. I thought, she was an unwanted kitten, put in an orphanage. I broke curses like, "Great, that's all we need, another cat." I broke curses of rejection, and I asked the Lord to bless her and give her a long life. I broke curses like, "Black cats mean bad luck," etc. I think the Holy Spirit was just bringing all these things to my mind. I started to picture her as an adult cat, living in my house. I asked the Lord to send ministering angels to Gracie (Hebrews 1:13-14) and to surround my house with angels who would cut off any enemy powers who would try to continue to distress the cat.

After my walk, I started to work on my computer on some worship overheads for the church. The thought entered my mind, "Anoint her with oil and pray" (Mark 6:13). So, I got some olive oil and did that the next three nights.

Friday, I had to take her back to the vet because she was still in bad shape. As I was driving her there, I prayed for protection from any words or curses spoken against her. That day I had to spend a lot of time in my car delivering Christmas presents to clients, so I kept praying in English and tongues and singing songs to the Lord, whatever came to my mind. As I would pray, I would reaffirm out loud that Gracie was going to live and not die, and I was going to proclaim the works of the Lord for her (Psalm 118:17). I said out loud that I believed she was going to get well and live, and to let it be unto me according to my faith (Matthew 9:29). I continued to rebuke and get angry at the thoughts that were plaguing me that she was going to die. I became like the woman who kept troubling the judge (Luke 18:1-8) or like the friend who keeps knocking on their neighbor's door in the middle of the night (Luke 11:5-13). The Holy Spirit was faithful to bring Scriptures to my remembrance (John 14:26).

Saturday, I was on my own, the vet couldn't take care of her. I think there was some doubt in the vet's eyes that she would last the weekend. I had paid close attention to the instructions on how to feed her and give her medicine, and kept walking in my faith that she would come out of this. But it seemed like the enemy was trying to thwart my every good intention, such as with the humidifier incident, and the incident earlier in the week where I overfed her. Saturday was also the day she went into the convulsions. When I would see the convulsions, I would go into a panic and start calling on the name of Jesus. I would say, "Jesus, You said if we called on Your name, we would be saved, so save me!" (Acts 2:21). And He did.

That night, I had to go to my company Christmas party. I really struggled with this because I knew I had to watch her to prevent her from going into convulsions. But I had to go to the party, so I just prayed, thanked (Eph. 5:20), rebuked, commanded, demanded, etc. When I came home, she was fine, but I just couldn't bear to watch the breathing difficulty continue. I was concerned again about her lasting the night. Another thought entered my head: what if she suffocates tonight from all her congestion? I commanded the demon of suffocation to leave her alone and not even dare to come near. Then I thought about a teaching my mother had about the spirit of Lilith, the demon that causes "crib death" or SIDS (sudden infant death syndrome). I thought, well, Gracie is a baby, so, I rebuked that spirit as well. The next morning, she was alive!

Sunday, she seemed even a little more alert, yet she still hadn't eaten on her own. By early afternoon, though, we threw a little rabbit-hair mouse to her, and she grabbed it in her mouth and wouldn't let me have it. In fact, my sweet, skinny little kitty started growling and hissing at me! My mom said, "I think she's hungry!" I put out some food for her and she devoured it! Praise God! She ate like a pig the next four days.

I took her back to the vet a week later. They were amazed! They said, "That's not the same cat!" She had gained 12 ounces in a week, almost 1/3 of her body weight the week before.

I still kept wondering why the Lord would not just instantly heal her, and dry up all the liquid that was causing her all the breathing problems, etc. And I wondered why it was the same thing with His children. Why sometimes instant, miraculous things happen in the areas of healings and sometimes they take more time. I don't know the answer, but the thought came to my mind that in the area of healing, we have to use our spirit to do our spiritual warfare for our soul for what we can't see with our physical eyes, and then we have to treat the physical things in our body that we see with our physical eyes, since we are composed of body, soul and spirit. So healings, in some cases, can take longer than we'd like because we're dealing with soul AND body. We have to govern both areas. Whereas, many times with instant miracles, perhaps we're only dealing more heavily with soulish and spiritual issues than we are with bodily issues, even though the body may be affected. I just kept thinking about that book I had recently read by Dodie Osteen where she fought daily with her cancer and was healed over a period of time by never giving in or giving up.

All my prayers and spiritual warfare against the enemy had worked. My faith had worked (as my mom said, I was "exercising my faith"). I give The Lord all the glory for His wonderful works (Psalm 107).

My sweet kitty turned from my little stuffy-nosed angel into a little hellion in the house! She's into everything! He strengthened my kitty: "But the Lord is faithful, and he will strengthen and protect you from the evil one" (II Thessalonians 3:3).

This incident was a valuable lesson to me in prolonged spiritual warfare—how to walk in faith and fight the enemy. Sometimes we can't have the immediate results we desire; that is why patience is a fruit of the Spirit (Gal. 5:22), and why we should trust God (Psalm 62:8). And that's why we should never remove our spiritual armor (Ephesians 6:10-18), because like it or not, we are in a daily warfare with the enemy until Jesus returns.

Amen! Even so, come Lord Jesus! (Rev. 22:20)

3

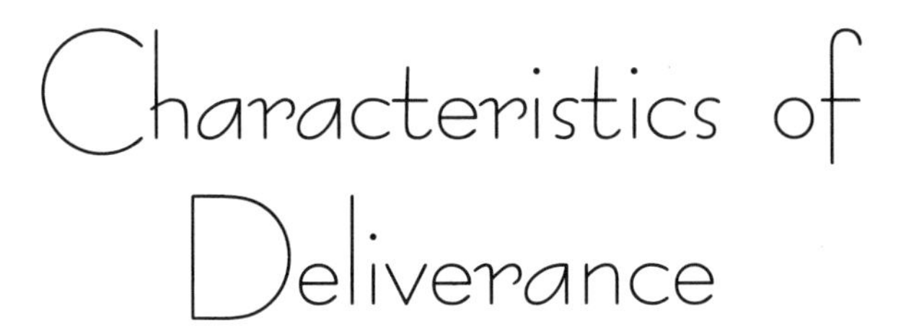

What Is Deliverance?

A. Deliverance is a commandment of the Lord Jesus Christ to cast out demons.

Matthew 10:1
And when he had called unto him his twelve disciples, he gave them power against unclean spirits, to cast them out, and to heal all manner of sickness and all manner of disease.

Matthew 10:7-8
And as ye go, preach, saying, The kingdom of heaven is at hand. Heal the sick, cleanse the lepers, raise the dead, cast out devils: freely ye have received, freely give.

Mark 6:7
And he called unto him the twelve, and began to send them forth by two and two; and gave them power over unclean spirits;

Mark 6:12-13
And they went out, and preached that men should repent. And they cast out many devils, and anointed with oil many that were sick, and healed them.

B. Deliverance is a gift from God. Jesus obtained salvation, healing and deliverance for us on the cross.

Ephesians 4:8
Wherefore he saith, When he ascended up on high, he led captivity captive, and gave gifts unto men.

Suppose you wanted to give a gift to someone you love, and you purchased the gift with money that you could have used for something you needed. But, because of your love for that person, you preferred to go without and instead put all your money into your carefully chosen gift. How would you feel, if your loved one rejected your gift?

Are some of us creating this same sad scenario by rejecting the gift of deliverance? It seems that there are different maturity levels of faith and trust in the Lord and understanding of the Scriptures that directly affect whether a Christian will investigate and/or accept this gift. Some Christians are content with simply being saved, and that's where their Christian growth ends. Other, perhaps more mature Christians, take their faith to another level, believing for or seeking supernatural healing. However, if deliverance is offered as a possible solution, almost all Christians react negatively to the suggestion. No, they do not want it. Perhaps someone else might need it, but not them. Are these Christians rejecting a gift of God that was purchased with His blood?

C. Deliverance is a sign of the believer. It marks a believer. In other words, if a person ministers deliverance, that person is a believer. If you are not a believer, you cannot minister deliverance.

Mark 16:17
And these signs shall follow them that believe; In my name shall they cast out devils;

What Deliverance Is Not

The ministry of deliverance is not for the glory of the minister; it is for the glory of God. During the ministry of Jesus on this earth, the people of Israel who watched Jesus cast out demons glorified and praised God.

Luke 10:20
Notwithstanding in this rejoice not, that the spirits are subject unto you; but rather rejoice, because your names are written in heaven.

The ministry of deliverance is not for the minister to have the opportunity to be theatrical, impress the people watching him, or be the center of attention. I have seen ministers and evangelists making a big production of casting out a demon, screaming at the top of their voices with great gestures, and then proclaiming dramatically that the person was set free. Showmanship does not usually result in deliverance, but merely plays on the emotions of the congregation, causing the audience stand up and give an ovation.

The ministry of deliverance should not make the minister feel important or superior, or cause him or her to desire admiration. Some ministers would like to portray that they have a special "gift" or special "anointing" for deliverance that God gave them because of some quality that they have, when, in fact, every born-again Christian has the power to cast out demons.

A deliverance minister is not especially holy. A Christian could be in sin and still cast out demons. However, it behooves that Christian to repent. A Christian who is casting out demons needs to obey God in all His commandments so as not to give Satan any opportunity to come against him/her.

Some ministers think that ministering deliverance is an opportunity to SCREAM!. They think that the louder they scream, the more power they have over demons. Sometimes they even scream into the person's ear! This is a lack of consideration for the person under ministry. The only ones screaming should be the demons.

What Deliverance Will Not Do

Deliverance is not a substitute for holiness. It is not a substitute for putting down the works of the flesh or the casting down of imaginations. It will not do the work we ourselves have to do, of combating the desires of the flesh or resisting the devil. Deliverance is not an easy way out.

Deliverance is a complement of sanctification. Deliverance helps the saints who are already engaged in battle. But for those who do not want to use self-control, deliverance will not be effective or lasting, if it happens at all. When temptation comes the way of someone who has received deliverance who really does not want to resist it, this person will fall into its trap again, and the demons will re-enter (and maybe worse ones). The person's attitude, thoughts, and desires hold the door open or closed to demons.

Why Should We Learn About Deliverance?

Some people do not want to hear about deliverance because of fear or because the demons (or their works) are repulsive. They indeed are.

When I was in school, I found Biology repulsive. Yet, I had to study it to get a well-balanced education. Besides, I would not have been able to graduate and receive a diploma.

If you were a king and an enemy waged war against you, you would need to study your enemy, know how he operates, know the weapons he uses, his tactics, etc., in order to war effectively against him. Otherwise you might lose your kingdom and be taken captive.

Satan and his demons are our enemy. We are in a battlefield whether we like it or not, and whether we know it or not. If we are at war, should we not study our enemies? Should we not learn all we can about them? Do we win wars by waiting to be attacked by the enemy and then merely defending ourselves? Do not think that because you do not know about the danger, you are safe. There is no point in trying to ignore the enemy.

What Does The Word of God Say About Knowledge?

Hosea 4:6
My people are destroyed for lack of knowledge: because thou hast rejected knowledge, I will also reject thee, that thou shalt be no priest to me: seeing thou hast forgotten the law

of thy God, I will also forget thy children.

Isaiah 5:13
Therefore my people are gone into captivity, because they have no knowledge: and their honourable men are famished, and their multitude dried up with thirst.

Isaiah 28:9
Whom shall he teach knowledge? and whom shall he make to understand doctrine? them that are weaned from the milk, and drawn from the breasts.

Hebrews 5:13-14
For every one that useth milk is unskilful in the word of righteousness: for he is a babe. But strong meat belongeth to them that are of full age, even those who by reason of use have their senses exercised to discern both good and evil.

Hebrews 6:1-3
Therefore leaving the principles of the doctrine of Christ, let us go on unto perfection; not laying again the foundation of repentance from dead works, and of faith toward God, Of the doctrine of baptisms, and of laying on of hands, and of resurrection of the dead, and of eternal judgment. And this will we do, if God permit.

2 Peter 1:5
And beside this, giving all diligence, add to your faith virtue; and to virtue knowledge;

Ephesians 6:12
For we wrestle not against flesh and blood, but against principalities, against powers, against the rulers of the darkness of this world, against spiritual wickedness in high places.

Upon This Rock

In the church, there are those who ignore the enemy. The enemy comes against them and they do not even know who hit them. There are others who are a little more informed and know who the enemy is, so when the enemy hits them, they know what is happening and can pinpoint the source of the trouble. But they do not know how to defend themselves. Then, there are others who know how to defend themselves against the attacks of Satan, and they are in a better position than the others.

However, this is not all that the Lord has planned for His church. The church is not supposed to be in a defensive position against Satan.

I was born in Cuba, and I lived in Havana. Havana was at one time a fortified city. It had great walls of stone surrounding it that had openings with reinforced gates that led out to the countryside. Two or three military forts defended the city, and at 9:00 p.m. one of them would fire a cannon as a signal to close the gates for the night for security. When pirates would land and try to sack the city, the cannon would signal to close the gates. The invaders were unsuccessful in their invasion until they could tear down at least one of the gates. If the gate resisted, and they could not tear it down, they could not accomplish their purpose and retreated.

Matthew 16:17-18
And Jesus answered and said unto him, Blessed art thou, Simon Bar-jonah: for flesh and blood hath not revealed it unto thee, but my Father which is in heaven. And I say also unto thee, That thou art Peter, and upon this rock I will build my church; and the gates of hell shall not prevail against it.

What did Jesus mean when He said, "The gates of Hell shall not prevail against my church"?

It means that we, His church, are not expected to be in a defensive position, but rather in an offensive position. In other words, we are expected to be storming hell, ramrodding its gates, and sacking it. He already said that the gates of Hell would not prevail against His church.

Then, why are we, at best, in a defensive position? Why is most of the church so ignorant about Satan and his demons, his wiles, his plans, his modus operandi, when Jesus' church is expected not only to know how to defend itself, but also to attack, attack, attack?

This ignorant, careless attitude was certainly not the attitude of the early church:

2 Corinthians 2:11
Lest Satan should get an advantage of us: for we are not ignorant of his devices.

Are we, as a church, in an army with a few generals and millions of foot soldiers, who do not even know that they are at war, and are continuously wounded, and do not even know why?

4

Demons

What Is A Demon?

Demons are evil spirits who work for Satan, can live in the air, and enter the spirit, soul and/or body of a human being when they can. They also can enter or inhabit animals and objects, including statues, furniture, houses, etc.

Their mission is to make life very difficult for human beings, and their final goal is to take us to hell.

Demons have personalities and acquire names. They are proud and arrogant, and they lie.

Demons prefer that humans ignore them. They prefer that humans not believe they exist. If they cannot stop humans from believing in their existence, then they would prefer that humans be frightened of them. This way, no one would interfere with their evil plans.

Demons Talk To Your Mind

The major battlefield of demons in a human being is the mind. Demons communicate to humans through their minds. How do demons talk to your mind? Have you ever had a thought that you wondered about? Maybe for an instant you wondered where the idea came from. Or maybe the idea was so ugly that you were ashamed of it and would not comment on it with anyone, because, of course, you believed it was your own thought. Demons delight when you believe their ideas are your own ideas. If you accept the wrong thought as being yours, then demons will add a string of related ideas and reasonings to it. When they have the person firmly convinced of those false ideas, they have created a stronghold.

The apostle Paul better explains it in the following Scripture:

2 Corinthians 10:3-5
For though we walk in the flesh, we do not war after the flesh: (For the weapons of our warfare are not carnal, but mighty through God to the pulling down of strong holds;) Casting down imaginations, and every high thing that exalteth itself against the knowledge of God, and bringing into captivity every thought to the obedience of Christ;

Where Do Demons Come From?

Today, no one knows what the origin of demons is. The Bible does not explain it. If the Lord Jesus Christ explained it to the disciples, it did not get recorded. There are doctrines and opinions, but the study of the origin of demons should not lead to arguments, because it is not important. Being concerned about their origin could distract us from the important point: casting them out. We have been commanded to cast them out and this is where we have to put our effort and time.

First theory. The theory that has most acceptance in the church today is the following: Lucifer was an archangel that covered the throne of God. Because he was beautiful and very talented especially in music, he became proud and thought himself equal to God. He incited a rebellion among the angels. God cast him down to Earth with the angels who had rebelled, which was one third of all the angels. His name was changed to Satan, and the rebellious angels are now called demons. The following Scriptures are the basis for this theory:

Ezekiel 28:12-19
Son of man, take up a lamentation upon the king of Tyrus, and say unto him, thus saith the Lord God; Thou sealest up the sum, full of wisdom, and perfect in beauty. Thou hast been in Eden the garden of God; every precious stone was thy covering, the sardius, topaz, and the diamond, the Beryl, the onyx, and the jasper, the sapphire, the emerald, and the carbuncle, and gold: the workmanship of thy tabrets and of thy pipes was prepared in thee in the day that thou wast created. Thou art the anointed cherub that covereth; and I have set thee so: thou wast upon the holy mountain of God; thou hast walked up and down in the midst of the stones of fire. Thou wast perfect in thy ways from the day that thou wast created, till iniquity was found in thee. By the multitude of thy merchandise they have filled the midst of thee with violence, and thou hast sinned: therefore I will cast thee as profane out of the mountain of God: and I will destroy thee, O covering cherub, from the midst of the stones of fire. Thine

heart was lifted up because of thy beauty, thou hast corrupted thy wisdom by reason of thy brightness: I will cast thee to the ground, I will lay thee before kings, that they may behold thee. Thou hast defiled thy sanctuaries by the multitude of thine iniquities, by the iniquity of thy traffick; therefore will I bring forth a fire from the midst of thee, it shall devour thee, and I will bring thee to ashes upon the earth in the sight of all them that behold thee. All they that know thee among the people shall be astonished at thee: thou shalt be a terror, and never shalt thou be any more.

Isaiah 14:12-17

How art thou fallen from heaven, O Lucifer, son of the morning! how art thou cut down to the ground, which didst weaken the nations! For thou hast said in thine heart, I will ascend into heaven, I will exalt my throne above the stars of God: I will sit also upon the mount of the congregation, in the sides of the north: I will ascend above the heights of the clouds; I will be like the most High.

They that see thee shall narrowly look upon thee, and consider thee, saying, Is this the man that made the earth to tremble, that did shake kingdoms; That made the world as a wilderness, and destroyed the cities thereof; that opened not the house of his prisoners?

Isaiah 24:21

And it shall come to pass in that day, that the Lord shall punish the host of the high ones that are on high, and the kings of the earth upon the earth.

Revelation 12:4

And his tail drew the third part of the stars of heaven, and did cast them to the earth: and the dragon stood before the woman which was ready to be delivered, for to devour her child as soon as it was born.

Revelation 12:7-9
And there was war in heaven: Michael and his angels fought against the dragon; and the dragon fought and his angels, And prevailed not; neither was their place found any more in heaven. And the great dragon was cast out, that old serpent, called the Devil, and Satan, which deceiveth the whole world: he was cast out into the earth, and his angels were cast out with him.

Second theory. This theory has been circulating for many years. It says that God created the heavens and the earth and populated the earth with men. These men sinned, so God destroyed the earth and its population. However, the souls of those evil men stayed around the earth (Genesis 1:1). The earth was in that state of destruction in Genesis 1:2. Then God re-created the earth and created Adam. The souls of the evil men who populated the first earth are the demons of today. The following Scriptures are the basis for this theory:

Genesis 1:2
And the earth was without form, and void; and darkness was upon the face of the deep. And the Spirit of God moved upon the face of the waters.

The word "was" in Hebrew is the word "haya" which should have been translated "became." It should read: *"And the earth became without form, and void...."* It also says that the earth was flooded: *"And the spirit of God moved upon the waters...."*

When God created the earth in Genesis 1:1, it was perfect, not shapeless and void as in Genesis 1:2. Everything that God does is perfect:

Psalms 18:30
As for God, <u>his way is perfect</u>: the word of the Lord is tried: he is a buckler to all those that trust in him.

Deuteronomy 32:4
He is the Rock, <u>his work is perfect</u>: for all his ways are judgment: a God of truth and without iniquity, just and right is he.

Isaiah 45:18
For thus saith the Lord that created the heavens; God himself that formed the earth and made it; he hath established it, <u>he created it not in vain, he formed it to be inhabited</u>: I am the Lord; and there is none else.

Ecclesiastes 3:11
<u>He hath made every thing beautiful in his time</u>: also he hath set the world in their heart, so that no man can find out the work that God maketh from the beginning to the end.

God was very angry when He decided to destroy the first earth:

Job 9:4-7
He is wise in heart, and mighty in strength: who hath hardened himself against him, and hath prospered? Which removeth the mountains, and they know not: which overturneth them in his anger.
Which shaketh the earth out of her place, and the pillars thereof tremble. Which commandeth the sun, and it riseth not; and sealeth up the stars.

Jeremiah 4:23-26
I beheld the earth, and, lo, it was without form, and void; and the heavens, and they had no light. I beheld the mountains, and, lo, they trembled, and all the hills moved

lightly. I beheld, and, lo, there was no man, and all the birds of the heavens were fled. I beheld, and, lo, the fruitful place was a wilderness, and all the cities thereof were broken down at the presence of the Lord, and by his fierce anger.

Isaiah 24:1
Behold, the Lord maketh the earth empty, and maketh it waste, and turneth it upside down, and scattereth abroad the inhabitants thereof.

These Scriptures describe the pre-Adamic flood, not Noah's:

Psalms 104:5-9
Who laid the foundations of the earth, that it should not be removed for ever. Thou coveredst it with the deep as with a garment: the waters stood above the mountains. At thy rebuke they fled; at the voice of thy thunder they hasted away. They go up by the mountains; they go down by the valleys unto the place which thou hast founded for them. Thou hast set a bound that they may not pass over; that they turn not again to cover the earth.

2 Peter 3:5-8
For this they willingly are ignorant of, that by the Word of God the heavens were of old, and the earth standing out of the water and in the water: Whereby the world that then was, being overflowed with water, perished: But the heavens and the earth, which are now, by the same word are kept in store, reserved unto fire against the day of judgment and perdition of ungodly men. But, beloved, be not ignorant of this one thing, that one day is with the Lord as a thousand years, and a thousand years as one day.

Third theory. The third theory is even older than the second. This theory is the one held by the Jews in Jesus' times.

The patriarch Enoch was known by the Jews as an author whose writings had a great circulation. In some circles, these writings were accepted as Scripture. In the book of Jude, Jude quotes Enoch from one of his writings:

Jude 1:14-15

And Enoch also, the seventh from Adam, prophesied of these, saying, Behold, the Lord cometh with ten thousands of his saints, To execute judgment upon all, and to convince all that are ungodly among them of all their ungodly deeds which they have ungodly committed, and of all their hard speeches which ungodly sinners have spoken against him.

The apocryphal book, *I Enoch*, says that the "sons of God" (Genesis 6:2) were angels who came to earth, called "watchers." They were 200 in number and had 20 leaders. These angels came with the assignment of teaching the men on earth about science, arts and crafts, but after a time, they desired the women on earth and took them for wives, disobeying God. They taught men how to make swords, jewelry, and cosmetics. They also taught astrology and witchcraft. They had children with the women, and these children grew to be very tall giants.

The giants wanted to eat meat, which was forbidden in those days. They started killing animals to eat their meat and drink their blood, and then they started killing men also to devour them. The angels above saw all the blood on the earth and told God. Because of the spilled blood and because of the fornication, God sent the flood (Noah's) to destroy all the people, including the giants.

Quote from the book: "The giants, evil spirits they will be on earth, and spirits of the evil ones they will be called. And the dwelling of the spirits of heaven is in heaven, but the dwelling of the spirits of earth, who were born on earth, is on earth."

The angels called watchers are also called fallen angels, and they are kept in chains. Several chapters of the book *I Enoch* are devoted to this story and to the punishment the angels received.

2 Peter 2:4-5
For if God spared not the angels that sinned, but cast them down to hell, and delivered them into chains of darkness, to be reserved unto judgment; And spared not the old world, but saved Noah the eighth person, a preacher of righteousness, bringing in the flood upon the world of the ungodly...

The three theories seem reasonable. But as I said, the origin of demons is not important. What is important is to cast them out, because we have orders to do so.

Demons in Different Cultures

Beings endowed with supernatural powers appear in the history and folklore of different cultures. They are described with different looks and given different names. For instance, in Spain they are called "genios," which is the same name the Romans called them: "genius." The trolls are from Denmark, Norway and Sweden. In Arab countries they are called "jinns." In Greece they are "lamias," in Japan they are "onis," etc. Fairies and gnomes are demons also.

Objections And Criticisms To The Deliverance Ministry

I have heard many objections and criticisms directed toward the deliverance ministry. These have not come from pagans, atheists, witches, or the world in general, but from Christians, the majority of which are pastors. The most common attacks are the following:

- Deliverance is of the Devil. It is demonic. You are getting involved with demons.
- Christians do not have demons. You should not minister to Christians. If you had demons cast out of you, you are not a Christian.
- We do not allow anyone to minister deliverance here!

- We do not allow the demons to scream or talk. We do not allow them to call attention to themselves.

- A battle is not necessary. There's something wrong with your ministry if you have to spend so much effort casting out demons. All you have to say is, "Come out in Jesus' name," and it is done.

- Only one word is needed. You do not need to talk so much. Demons come out with only one word.

- Deliverance should not take so long; it should be instant. That's the way Jesus did it, instantly.

- You are out of balance, because all you talk about is deliverance, and all you do is deliverance.

- We should not scare the congregation. They are not ready yet. Don't talk about deliverance.

- We do not want to hear testimonies of deliverance here.

All these objections have come from people who should know better, because they claim to know the Word of God. Yet even when they supposedly know the Word of God, they have never ministered deliverance, and they really do not know how it is done. A focused study of the deliverance ministry of Jesus would give these critics a better understanding of the deliverance ministry.

In this chapter we will analyze the pertinent Scriptures to find truthful answers to objections. If you enter the deliverance ministry, this chapter will help you give scriptural answers to the critics you will encounter.

Study 1: A Demon In the Synagogue

Mark 1:21-27

And they went into Capernaum; and straightway on the sabbath day he entered into the synagogue, and taught. And they were astonished at his doctrine: for he taught them as one that had authority, and not as the scribes. And there was in their synagogue a man with an unclean spirit; and he cried out, Saying, Let us alone; what have we to do with thee, thou Jesus of Nazareth? art thou come to destroy us? I know thee who thou art, the Holy One of God. And Jesus rebuked him, saying, Hold thy peace, and come out of him. And when the unclean spirit had torn him, and cried with a loud voice, he came out of him. And they were all amazed, insomuch that they questioned among themselves, saying, What thing is this? what new doctrine is this? for with authority commandeth he even the unclean spirits, and they do obey him.

Luke 4:31-37

And came down to Capernaum, a city of Galilee, and taught them on the sabbath days. And they were astonished at his doctrine: for his word was with power. And in the synagogue there was a man, which had a spirit of an unclean devil, and cried out with a loud voice, Saying, Let us alone; what have we to do with thee, thou Jesus of Nazareth? art thou come to destroy us? I know thee who thou art; the Holy One of God. And Jesus rebuked him, saying, Hold thy peace, and come out of him. And when the devil had thrown him in the midst, he came out of him, and hurt him not. And they were all amazed, and spake among themselves, saying, What a word is this! for with authority and power he commandeth the unclean spirits, and they come out. And the fame of him went out into every place of the country round about.

Questions:

- What day of the week did this happen?
- Where did it happen?
- What was Jesus doing there?
- What happened when Jesus started?
- Did the demon talk?
- How loud did it talk?
- What two questions did the demon ask?
- What did the demon state afterwards?
- Did Jesus tell the demon to shut up?
- If so, why do you think He did it?
- After Jesus commanded the demon to come out, how many things did the demon do before coming out?
- What was the reaction of the people?
- What did the people say?
- Was this a private deliverance?
- Was this a quiet deliverance?

Jesus was at a synagogue and was teaching. Anointed teaching of the truth generally makes demons manifest in the congregation. Here the demon manifested screaming, but he was revealing who Jesus was. So Jesus commanded the demon to shut up and to leave.

Note that the man in whom the demon manifested was attending the Sabbath service at the synagogue; he was not a pagan. He was a nice Jewish boy!

The demon did not leave immediately. First, he took the time to "tear" the man and did some extra screaming besides. In the Gospel of Luke it says that the demon threw him to the floor in the middle of the people attending the service. This is quite a manifestation.

Jesus and the man were not asked to leave the synagogue so that the congregation would not be disturbed or frightened, which is what would happen in most churches today. Also, they were not scooted away to a private room. The deliverance was done in full view and hearing of the congregation.

The people, instead of being scared as today's pastors say they would be, were amazed by the authority and power of Jesus, since He did not use any of the rituals, chants and objects used by exorcists.

Conclusions:
- Public deliverance was allowed in the synagogue.
- Loud manifestations were allowed.

Study 2: A Demonic Sickness

From the synagogue, Jesus goes to Peter's house to have dinner.

Mark 1:29-31
And forthwith, when they were come out of the synagogue, they entered into the house of Simon and Andrew, with James and John. But Simon's wife's mother lay sick of a fever, and anon they tell him of her. And he came and took her by the hand, and lifted her up; and immediately the fever left her, and she ministered unto them.

Matthew 8:14-15
And when Jesus was come into Peter's house, he saw his wife's mother laid, and sick of a fever. And he touched her hand, and the fever left her: and she arose, and ministered unto them.

Luke 4:38-39
And he arose out of the synagogue, and entered into Simon's house. And Simon's wife's mother was taken with a great

fever; and they besought him for her. And he stood over her, and rebuked the fever; and it left her: and immediately she arose and ministered unto them.

Questions:

- Where was Jesus when He ministered?
- What did Peter's mother-in-law have?
- What did Jesus do?
- Was it an immediate result?

Jesus entered a private home and was led to a woman sick in bed with a fever. He was asked to heal her. He took her by the hand and **rebuked** the fever. She immediately was healed and her strength returned. Then, she went about her business. Because he rebuked the fever, it was a deliverance. It indicates that the sickness was caused by demons only. Sickness can be all purely physical, for which healing should be ministered. It can be all demonic, for which deliverance should be ministered. And it can be a combination of the two, for which both healing and deliverance should be ministered.

Rebuke: A sharp reprimand; a chiding; reproof for faults; reprehension *(Webster's Unabridged Dictionary*).

Rebuke: *Strong's Dictionary*, word #2008, censure or admonish, forbid, charge.

Conclusions:

- A sickness that was totally provoked by demons.
- Deliverance ministered at a private home.

Study 3: Deliverance Ministered On The Sidewalk

The people of Capernaum who saw what had happened in the synagogue in the morning told others, and they found out where Jesus was staying. They were very excited and brought those who were sick or tormented to Jesus. They came through the streets in the dark, with oil lamps in their hands, all the way to Peter's house. Jesus had to sit at the door of the house to be able to minister to them, and since there were no front gardens or yards, He was sitting right on the public street.

Mark 1:32-33
And at even, when the sun did set, they brought unto him all that were diseased, and them that were possessed with devils. And all the city was gathered together at the door.

Matthew 8:16
When the even was come, they brought unto him many that were possessed with devils: and he cast out the spirits with his word, and healed all that were sick:

Luke 4:40-41
Now when the sun was setting, all they that had any sick with divers diseases brought them unto him; and he laid his hands on every one of them, and healed them. And devils also came out of many, crying out, and saying, Thou art Christ the Son of God. And he rebuking them suffered them not to speak: for they knew that he was Christ.

Questions:

- Where was Jesus while He was ministering?
- In the Gospel of Matthew, how does it say that He cast out the demons?
- How did He heal?

- Did He tell the demons not to talk?
- What was the reason that He did not want the demons to talk?
- Were these private deliverances?

The objection, "only one word is needed," is based in this Scripture in Matthew, and indeed some translations say "one word" instead of "His word."

The Greek word used here for "word" is "logos." The Greek dictionary says that *logos* (#3056 in *Strong's Concordance*) means something said, a topic (subject of discourse), reasoning or motive, a computation, account, cause, communication, doctrine, preaching, question, reason, say, speaker, speech, talk, tidings, treatise, utterance, word, work.

So, Jesus cast out demons with what He said, His account, His doctrine, His preaching, His speech, His talk, His tidings, His work. Not just one word!

In this Scripture, Jesus cast out demons on the street, in front of the house. He never took people to a private place to give them deliverance. It was always in public.

The only time that He commanded the demons to be silent was when they were revealing, in front of everyone, that He was the Christ. That was His <u>only</u> reason to shut the demons up. In other Scriptures we will see that He allowed the demons to talk.

Conclusions:

- He ministered deliverance with His speech and His preaching.
- He ministered openly out in the public street.
- The only time He forbade the demons to talk was when they were saying that He was the Messiah.

Study 4: All The Synagogues Of Galilee

Mark 1:38-39

And he said unto them, Let us go into the next towns, that I may preach there also: for therefore came I forth. And he preached in their synagogues throughout all Galilee and cast out devils.

Questions:

- Where did Jesus go?
- What did He do in the synagogues?
- How many synagogues did He go to?

Jesus preached and cast out demons in all the synagogues of Galilee. How many churches do you know of where demons are cast out after the preaching is concluded?

He was allowed to minister both healing and deliverance, with demons manifesting and crying out, as we have seen in the previous Scriptures. Today, the vast majority of churches do not want demons cast out during services or otherwise. The pastors need to ask themselves: WWJD?

Conclusions:

- All the synagogues allowed deliverance during their services.

Study 5: At The Foot Of The Mountain

Matthew 4:24

And his fame went throughout all Syria: and they brought unto him all sick people that were taken with divers diseases and torments, and those which were possessed with devils, and those which were lunatick, and those that had the palsy; and he healed them.

Luke 6:17-18

And he came down with them, and stood in the plain, and the company of his disciples, and a great multitude of people out of all Judaea and Jerusalem, and from the sea coast of Tyre and Sidon, which came to hear him, and to be healed of their diseases; And they that were vexed with unclean spirits: and they were healed.

Questions:

- What kind of problems did the people who were brought to Him have?
- Where was He when ministering to the people?
- Did He make private appointments?
- Was the ministry of healing and deliverance private?

Jesus conducted a public ministry of healing and deliverance at the foot of a mountain, in the open air of the countryside. Jesus had gone to the mountain to pray in order to select His disciples. He came down with them and found a level place on the side of the mountain. The people again brought to Him the sick and those vexed with demons, and He healed them all right there where He was. No one requested "privacy."

Conclusion:

- Another example of Jesus ministering healing and deliverance openly and publicly, this time in the countryside.

Study 6: "You Are The Son Of God"

Mark 3:7, 9, 11, 12

But Jesus withdrew himself with his disciples to the sea: and a great multitude from Galilee followed him, and from Judaea..... And he spake to his disciples, that a small ship should wait on him because of the multitude, lest they should throng him...And unclean spirits, when they saw him, fell down before him, and cried, saying, Thou art the Son of God. And he straitly charged them that they should not make him known.

Questions:

- Where was He?
- Were demons manifesting?
- Did the demons talk?
- Did Jesus tell them to shut up?
- Why did He tell them to shut up?

Jesus was by the sea side, and as the multitude grew, He had to get on a boat. From the shore, people would manifest demons that threw them to the ground and screamed saying, "You are the Son of God!" Because they were revealing Him as the Messiah, Jesus commanded them to be silent.

I picture Him standing on the boat, with someone rowing the boat slowly along the shore while He was preaching, so that He could preach to the people spread along the shore. As the boat approached, the demons would start manifesting.

Conclusions:

- Deliverance ministered in public and openly.
- Demons not allowed to talk because they were saying Jesus was the Messiah.

Study 7: In Danger Of Blaspheming The Holy Spirit

Mark 3:22-26

And the scribes which came down from Jerusalem said, He hath Beelzebub, and by the prince of the devils casteth he out devils. And he called them unto him, and said unto them in parables, How can Satan cast out Satan? And if a kingdom be divided against itself, that kingdom cannot stand. And if a house be divided against itself, that house cannot stand. And if Satan rise up against himself, and be divided, he cannot stand, but hath an end.

Matthew 12:22-28
Then was brought unto him one possessed with a devil, blind, and dumb: and he healed him, insomuch that the blind and dumb both spake and saw. And all the people were amazed, and said, Is not this the son of David? But when the Pharisees heard it, they said, This fellow doth not cast out devils, but by Beelzebub the prince of the devils.

And Jesus knew their thoughts, and said unto them, Every kingdom divided against itself is brought to desolation; and every city or house divided against itself shall not stand: And if Satan cast out Satan, he is divided against himself; how shall then his kingdom stand? And if I by Beelzebub cast out devils, by whom do your children cast them out? therefore they shall be your judges. But if I cast out devils by the Spirit of God, then the kingdom of God is come unto you.

Scribes: Members of a learned class in ancient Israel through New Testament times who studied the Scriptures and served as copyists, editors and teachers.

Pharisees: A religious and political party in Palestine in New Testament times. The Pharisees were known for insisting that the law of God be observed as the scribes interpreted it, and for their special commitment to keeping the laws of tithing and ritual purity.

(*Illustrated Dictionary of the Bible*, Herbert Lockyer, Thomas Nelson Publishers)

Questions:

- What was the real problem with the blind and dumb man?
- What was the reaction of the people when Jesus healed him?
- Who did the people think that Jesus was?
- Who criticized Jesus for casting out demons?
- What kind of power did they say Jesus used to cast out demons?
- Did Jesus know what they were thinking?

A blind and dumb man was brought to Jesus. He had a disease or defect that was caused by demons. When Jesus cast the demons out, therefore healing the man, the "lay" people were amazed and realized that He was the son of David, the Messiah. But when the theologians heard the people saying that He was the Messiah, they accused Jesus of having a "familiar spirit" or "spirit guide" that gave Him the power (through Beelzebub) to cast out demons.

Still today, some people think that if you cast out demons, you are operating in witchcraft.

Several years ago, when I was still working in architecture and commercial interior design, a Jewish architect, whom I had befriended tried to persuade me for years to close my own interior design business and work for him. He knew I was a born-again Christian, but he did not know that I ministered deliverance. I eventually closed my business, and when he heard about it, he proposed that I start an interior design department at his architectural office. I went to work for him. Eventually, I told him that I had a ministry of deliverance. This apparently disturbed him, because he called a person whom he respected, who was either a pastor or an elder, to ask his opinion about what I told him.

The man told him that what I was doing "was demonic." My architect friend could not have me around any longer, and I had to leave my job. This shows that the spirit of the Pharisees is still in the world today, as are all the demons of antiquity.

Satan does not want demons to be cast out of human beings. Demons are eager to be in people, to use their souls and bodies to kill, steal and destroy. They are commissioned by Satan to engage in destruction, sickness, chaos, perversion, confusion and murder. Why would Satan want to drive a demon out of a human when he works full-time at demonizing people? For someone to say that Christians cast out demons by the power of Satan is the farthest from the truth that anyone can be.

Luke 10:19-20
Behold, I give unto you power to tread on serpents and scorpions, and over all the power of the enemy: and nothing shall by any means hurt you. Notwithstanding in this rejoice not, that the spirits are subject unto you; but rather rejoice, because your names are written in heaven.

It is true that some witches, curanderos and exorcists cast demons out, but they are never able to get the person entirely free. They are the ones who do deliverance by the powers of darkness, casting one demon out of the person and helping another demon enter the person.

Conclusions:

- The blindness and dumbness was caused by a demon.
- The lay people had more discernment than the religious people.
- No one who casts demons out in the name of Jesus casts demons out through demonic power.

Study 8: The Stronghold

Mark 3:27
No man can enter into a strong man's house, and spoil his goods, except he will first bind the strong man; and then he will spoil his house.

Matthew 12:29
Or else how can one enter into a strong man's house, and spoil his goods, except he first bind the strong man? and then he will spoil his house.

What is a strong man or stronghold? The strong man guards a stronghold. For the purpose of deliverance, the strong man and the stronghold are practically the same.

Have you ever seen a policeman overcome a criminal and put him in handcuffs in real life or on TV? You saw the policeman "binding the strong man." Binding the strongman means overcoming him by force and making sure that he is rendered powerless.

A bank may have an armed guard to protect it from hold-ups. He is the strong man in the bank. If you would like to steal some money from the bank, you know that you have to overcome and bind the guard, so that you can get into the vault and cart the money away.

The word "bind" in *Strong's Concordance* is #1210, and means be in bonds, knit (as knotting), tie.

We do not rob banks, but sometimes when we go to "spoil a house" (cast demons out of their "house," a person), we find strong opposition from a "strongman" that is guarding what is inside.

2 Corinthians 10:3-5
For though we walk in the flesh, we do not war after the flesh: (For the weapons of our warfare are not carnal, but mighty through God to the pulling down of strong holds;) Casting down imaginations, and every high thing that exalteth itself against the knowledge of God, and bringing into captivity every thought to the obedience of Christ;

My definition of a stronghold in a person is the wrong idea, thought, concept or belief that the person has and wants to preserve. A stronghold is believing a lie. Who is the father of lies? Satan!

When there is a stronghold, it is because the person has believed a lie of Satan, and the person is convinced to believe the lie and not the truth. This lie might have been implanted in their mind by the demons in the person, or it might have been told to the person by his/her parents, or by a teacher, or by a pastor, or by a friend, all of them being used by Satan to convey the lie. The job of the deliverance minister in this case is to prove to the person that the belief is a lie. The person will not receive deliverance as long as he/she continues to believe the lie. The lie is the strong man, and you have to overcome it and render it powerless before you can get to the demons and cast them out. The demons will not even manifest while there is a stronghold. The demons feel very secure and snug in the stronghold. If you cannot convince the person that they are believing a lie, there will not be any deliverance.

Isaiah 44:20
He feedeth on ashes: a deceived heart hath turned him aside, that he cannot deliver his soul, nor say, Is there not a lie in my right hand?

Conclusion:

- To bind the strong man, you have to find out what lies have been believed, and then you have to guide the person to the truth. If the person realizes that he/she has been deceived, the strong man loses his power, and then you can cast the demons out.

Study 9: Rebuking Wind And Waves

Matthew 8:23-26

And when he was entered into a ship, his disciples followed him. And, behold, there arose a great tempest in the sea, insomuch that the ship was covered with the waves: but he was asleep. And his disciples came to him, and awoke him, saying, Lord, save us: we perish. And he saith unto them, Why are ye fearful, O ye of little faith? Then he arose, and rebuked the winds and the sea; and there was a great calm.

Mark 4:36-40

And when they had sent away the multitude, they took him even as he was in the ship. And there were also with him other little ships. And there arose a great storm of wind, and the waves beat into the ship, so that it was now full. And he was in the hinder part of the ship, asleep on a pillow: and they awake him, and say unto him, Master, carest thou not that we perish? And he arose, and rebuked the wind, and said unto the sea, Peace, be still. And the wind ceased, and there was a great calm. And he said unto them, Why are ye so fearful? how is it that ye have no faith?

Questions:

- Where were they going?
- Was this a destructive weather pattern?
- What happened to the disciples?
- What was Jesus doing?

- Did the disciples think Jesus could help?
- What did Jesus tell them when they awakened Him?
- Why do you think that Jesus was irritated? Do you think it was because He was awakened?
- What did Jesus do to calm the wind and the sea?

These Scriptures really do not have to do with personal deliverance, but they have to do with spiritual warfare. They are included because we have to learn about the authority we have in Christ Jesus "according to the power which works in us" (Ephesians 3:20).

The Lord and His disciples were in a boat sailing across the sea of Galilee to the coast of Gadara. Jesus was going to meet a very demonized man upon arriving to the coast of Gadara. It was not in Satan's best interest that Jesus meet this man. Satan provoked a storm to prevent the Lord and His disciples from reaching the coast.

The disciples were scared. Their faith in Jesus made them sure that Jesus would overcome the situation. However, when they woke Him up, it was obvious that the Lord esteemed that the disciples could have overcome the storm themselves. He accused them of not having faith.

Jesus "rebuked" the wind. This is the same word that Jesus used when healing Peter's mother-in-law. He rebuked her fever. Jesus knew that the fever had demonic roots. He also knew that the storm had demonic roots. The solution was the same: He "rebuked" them both with astonishing results.

Is it a surprise to you that storms could be induced by demons? Other cultures have known it and manipulate the weather for their convenience. The American Indian rain dances accomplish something; otherwise, the Indians would not have not wasted their time with them.

Religions from other cultures have gods (demons) that are in charge of thunder, lightning, wind, rain, and storms. Chango and Oxun are African gods of thunder and lightning, and they also appear in the Cuban Santeria religion. In the Greek and Roman religions, there are also gods of storms. Every pagan religion has gods of storms, thunder and lightning. They are all demons.

Witchcraft also tries to control or influence weather. There is a spiritual aspect to weather. Remember that God sent the flood, then sent the rainbow and promised not to send a worldwide flood again. He sent hail to Egypt. God sends droughts to rebellious people, and promises rain in due time to the obedient. God allows demons to manipulate weather, perhaps to test us to see if we will take the authority that He has given us and use it against bad weather. If we have faith, we will do it. On the Internet, find www.demonbuster.com/weather.html and print it. It will help you in praying against bad weather.

The Lord told me even before I entered the deliverance ministry to pray against storms and take authority over the clouds, the wind, the rain, the barometric pressure, the temperature and the vapors. I imagine the vapors are the evaporated water that goes up from the earth to form clouds. I take authority and command the weather to obey the Word of God of no flood and no destruction. I observe the weather maps on TV, and based on what I see storms doing, I command them to dissolve or weaken, to move quickly (not stall) on their path or veer slightly so as not to go over very populated areas. In extreme weather prayer warriors should study the weather map and come into agreement on how to pray.

Study 10: In The Graveyard

Matthew 8:28-34

And when he was come to the other side into the country of the Gergesenes, there met him two possessed with devils, coming out of the tombs, exceeding fierce, so that no man might pass by that way. And, behold, they cried out, saying, What have we to do with thee, Jesus, thou Son of God? art thou come hither to torment us before the time?

And there was a good way off from them an herd of many swine feeding. So the devils besought him, saying, If thou cast us out, suffer us to go away into the herd of swine. And he said unto them, Go. And when they were come out, they went into the herd of swine: and, behold, the whole herd of swine ran violently down a steep place into the sea, and perished in the waters.

And they that kept them fled, and went their ways into the city, and told every thing, and what was befallen to the possessed of the devils. And, behold, the whole city came out to meet Jesus: and when they saw him, they besought him that he would depart out of their coasts.

Mark 5:1-20

And they came over unto the other side of the sea, into the country of the Gadarenes. And when he was come out of the ship, immediately there met him out of the tombs a man with an unclean spirit,

Who had his dwelling among the tombs; and no man could bind him, no, not with chains: Because that he had been often bound with fetters and chains, and the chains had been plucked asunder by him, and the fetters broken in pieces: neither could any man tame him. And always, night and day,

he was in the mountains, and in the tombs, crying, and cutting himself with stones.
But when he saw Jesus afar off, he ran and worshipped him, And cried with a loud voice, and said, What have I to do with thee, Jesus, thou Son of the most high God? I adjure thee by God, that thou torment me not.

For he said unto him, Come out of the man, thou unclean spirit. And he asked him, What is thy name? And he answered, saying, My name is Legion: for we are many. And he besought him much that he would not send them away out of the country.

Now there was there nigh unto the mountains a great herd of swine feeding. And all the devils besought him, saying, Send us into the swine, that we may enter into them. And forthwith Jesus gave them leave. And the unclean spirits went out, and entered into the swine: and the herd ran violently down a steep place into the sea, (they were about two thousand;) and were choked in the sea.

And they that fed the swine fled, and told it in the city, and in the country. And they went out to see what it was that was done. And they come to Jesus, and see him that was possessed with the devil, and had the legion, sitting, and clothed, and in his right mind: and they were afraid. And they that saw it told them how it befell to him that was possessed with the devil, and also concerning the swine. And they began to pray him to depart out of their coasts.

And when he was come into the ship, he that had been possessed with the devil prayed him that he might be with him. Howbeit Jesus suffered him not, but saith unto him, Go home to thy friends, and tell them how great things the Lord hath done for thee, and hath had compassion on thee. And he departed, and began to publish in Decapolis how great things Jesus had done for him: and all men did marvel.

Luke 8:26-39

And they arrived at the country of the Gadarenes, which is over against Galilee. And when he went forth to land, there met him out of the city a certain man, which had devils long time, and ware no clothes, neither abode in any house, but in the tombs.

When he saw Jesus, he cried out, and fell down before him, and with a loud voice said, What have I to do with thee, Jesus, thou Son of God most high? I beseech thee, torment me not. (For he had commanded the unclean spirit to come out of the man. For oftentimes it had caught him: and he was kept bound with chains and in fetters; and he brake the bands, and was driven of the devil into the wilderness.)

And Jesus asked him, saying, What is thy name? And he said, Legion: because many devils were entered into him. And they besought him that he would not command them to go out into the deep.

And there was there an herd of many swine feeding on the mountain: and they besought him that he would suffer them to enter into them. And he suffered them. Then went the devils out of the man, and entered into the swine: and the herd ran violently down a steep place into the lake, and were choked.

When they that fed them saw what was done, they fled, and went and told it in the city and in the country. Then they went out to see what was done; and came to Jesus, and found the man, out of whom the devils were departed, sitting at the feet of Jesus, clothed, and in his right mind: and they were afraid. They also which saw it told them by what means he that was possessed of the devils was healed. Then the whole multitude of the country of the Gadarenes round about besought him to depart from them; for they were taken with

great fear: and he went up into the ship, and returned back again.
Now the man out of whom the devils were departed besought him that he might be with him: but Jesus sent him away, saying, Return to thine own house, and shew how great things God hath done unto thee. And he went his way, and published throughout the whole city how great things Jesus had done unto him.

Questions: (Use *Mark 5* for the answers. In this case, when I refer to the demon, I am talking about the demon that was talking to Jesus, not the entire legion under that demon.)

- Where was Gadara?
- Who were the Gadarenes?
- In what specific location was this deliverance performed?
- In your opinion, was this man possessed?
- What happened when the man saw Jesus?
- Did the demon speak?
- What did the demon say?
- Did Jesus tell the demon to shut up?
- If not, why do you think that He did not tell him to shut up this time?
- What did Jesus say to the man?
- Did the demon come out after Jesus said it?
- How much did the demons talk?
- How much time do you think passed before the demon came out with all the demons working under him?
- What were the Gadarenes raising?
- Why do you think the Gadarenes were raising them?
- What was the Gadarenes' reaction when they realized what happened?
- Why would they have those feelings?
- What did they tell Jesus to do?

- In your opinion, were the Gadarenes "children" or "seed" of Abraham?
- When Jesus was leaving, what did the healed man want to do?
- What did Jesus tell the man to do?
- Do you think that Jesus' command to the man is good for today? Should we do the same thing?

After calming the storm, Jesus and his disciples reach the coast of Gadara. The area of Gadara was named after the tribe of Gad. We need to remember a characteristic of the tribe of Gad: to reach the Promised Land, the children of Israel had to cross the Jordan river. (If you recall the map of Israel, you see the east border is delineated by the Jordan river. The Jordan river springs from the Sea of Galilee to the north and empties into the Dead Sea to the south.) When the children of Israel reached the Jordan river, the tribe of Gad did not want to cross over.

Numbers 32:1, 2, 4, 5

Now the children of Reuben and the children of Gad had a very great multitude of cattle: and when they saw the land of Gazer, and the land of Gilead, that, behold, the place was a place for cattle; The children of Gad and the children of Reuben came and spake unto Moses, and to Eleazar the priest, and unto the princes of the congregation, saying...Even the country which the Lord smote before the congregation of Israel, is a land for cattle, and thy servants have cattle: Wherefore, said they, if we have found grace in thy sight, let this land be given unto thy servants for a possession, and bring us not over Jordan.

The tribes of Reuben and Gad were allowed to leave the cattle, women and children on the other side of the river, while the men crossed the Jordan to help the other tribes possess the Promised Land. Then, they returned to settle on the other side of the river, which was not the Promised Land. They were disobedient. At the least, they could have gone to see the land on the other side of the river before making a decision. But they had seen the land that was spread before their eyes, and they liked it. They decided they wanted that land, against the perfect will of God. Their spirit of rebellion, disobedience and lack of submission to God was still manifesting in the area years later, as you will see shortly.

Deuteronomy 14:1-3,8
Ye are the children of the Lord your God: ye shall not cut yourselves, nor make any baldness between your eyes for the dead. For thou art an holy people unto the Lord thy God, and the Lord hath chosen thee to be a peculiar people unto himself, above all the nations that are upon the earth. Thou shalt not eat any abominable thing ... And the swine, because it divideth the hoof, yet cheweth not the cud, it is unclean unto you: ye shall not eat of their flesh, nor touch their dead carcase.

The children of Israel were prohibited from eating pork, much less use it for sacrifices. So, why were the Gadarenes raising pigs?

It is possible that in Jesus day there were no descendants of the tribe of Gad in Gadara since the ten tribes of the north had supposedly "disappeared" after their exile in Syria. Nevertheless, the spirit of disobedience was still over the area, since the worst demonization case we find in the Gospels lived in Gadara. Satan had some special designs for this area, since he did not want Jesus to reach this man, and this was the sole reason for the demonic storm that scared the disciples so much. This man, after being set free, preached the Gospel to the Gadarenes, and this is what Satan was trying to stop from happening with the storm.

Before his deliverance, this man was so wild that the people of the area were afraid of him and would not even pass that way. When Jesus and His disciples entered the graveyard, there was no one there except the man. Jesus knew the state of the man, and this is why commanding the demon out was the first thing he did. Then the demon started to shout and called Him "Son of God." Notice that Jesus did not tell the demon to shut up this time. Why? Because there was no other person to hear what the demon was saying, but His disciples.

The demon did not come out when Jesus commanded him. Instead, the demon asked Him if He had come to torment him before the time (before the time of the Lake of Fire). Jesus then asked his name, and the demon gave it. Then, the demon started negotiating with Jesus about where the legion would go. As you can see, the demon did not come out when Jesus commanded him to leave. On the contrary, he talked and negotiated before leaving, and that certainly took some time.

It is peculiar that when the people of Gadara approached the graveyard and found the man healed, they were greatly afraid. This is in contrast to the people on the other side of the Sea of Galilee, who marveled and praised God when they saw Jesus casting out demons. Why? The demons in the Gadarenes were the ones who were afraid. Most of the people of Gadara were heavily demonized because of disobedience and rebellion, which were the territorial demons over the area. They could not even praise God or thank Jesus for the deliverance of the man.

Multitudes on the other side of the river followed Jesus, bringing the sick and demonized to Him for healing. Instead, the Gadarenes wanted Jesus to leave the area as soon as possible. They could not stand to have the anointed of God near them. It bothered them, because the demons inside of them were terrified.

When a pastor says, "I do not want deliverance here because the congregation might get frightened," he does not know it, but what he is really saying is that the congregation might be harboring demons. People who are free will praise God when they see someone being set free.

Deliverance ministers sometimes also experience the rejection of certain people right in their own church. As soon as these people know that someone can cast out demons, they do not want anything to do with him/her. They go to extremes to avoid the deliverance minister, and they do not even greet him/her when passing by.

One final thing you need to notice in this Scripture is that Jesus told the man to go to his people and proclaim what God had done for him. This is what the Lord wants. If you have been healed or delivered, proclaim it!

Conclusions:

- Disobedience to the will of God opens the door to demons.
- Jesus talked to the demon.
- The demon did not come out instantly.
- The demon negotiated with Jesus.
- Jesus did not tell the demon to shut up.
- The Gadarenes wanted Jesus to leave because He cast out demons.
- Jesus wants whoever gets healed or delivered to proclaim it.

Study 11: He Could Not Talk

Matthew 9:32-34
As they went out, behold, they brought to him a dumb man possessed with a devil. And when the devil was cast out, the dumb spake: and the multitudes marvelled, saying, It was never so seen in Israel. But the Pharisees said, He casteth out devils through the prince of the devils.

Questions:

- Who do you think diagnosed the man as "possessed" with a devil?
- Was this an "instant" deliverance?
- Was this a "private" deliverance?
- What was the reaction of the people?
- What is the meaning of "never seen in Israel"?
- What was the reaction of the Pharisees?

"They" brought Jesus a man who was mute. I don't cease to be amazed, as I read the Gospels, at how the people of Israel could diagnose and know when illness or strange behavior was caused by a demon. Today, if I suggest that the cause of a physical incapacity is a demon, whoever hears me thinks that I am crazy or in need of professional counseling and therapy.

As the Scripture is written, it indicates that this demon took some time to leave: "And when..." does not indicate an instant deliverance.

I have seen an instant deliverance of a very strong Lucifer in which all the other demons present in the person came out along with the Lucifer demon. This was a miracle deliverance in a special circumstance which the Lord considered that it merited His appearance. When He appeared, the demons scrambled and left as fast as possible. The Lucifer was a power of the air that came to help the demon I was casting out from a former witch. Through a word of knowledge, the Lord gave the name of the demon: "It is a prince, it is Lucifer," and I believe it was Satan himself, whom the Lord still called Lucifer. This is the only "instant deliverance" that I have seen.

In the Scripture, the people marveled. They had not seen deliverance but only exorcism before. They were used to exorcisms, and this way of casting out demons was new to them.

The Pharisees had religious spirits. A spirit of religious jealousy made them say things that put them in danger of eternal damnation, because what they said was blasphemy against the Holy Spirit. Saying that Jesus was casting out demons through Satan instead of "by the finger of God" is blasphemy against the Holy Spirit.

Conclusions:

- Even when Jesus ministered, the demons would not come out instantly.
- The man was not able to speak, and the cause was a demon.
- Even when the people were acquainted with and could diagnose demons, they had never seen deliverance the way Jesus did it.
- The religious spirits reject deliverance.
- Anyone who attributes deliverance to the power of Satan is blaspheming the Holy Spirit.

Study 12: A Woman Of God Has A Demon

Luke 13:10-17

And he was teaching in one of the synagogues on the sabbath. And, behold, there was a woman which had a spirit of infirmity eighteen years, and was bowed together, and could in no wise lift up herself.

And when Jesus saw her, he called her to him, and said unto her, Woman, thou art loosed from thine infirmity. And he laid his hands on her: and immediately she was made straight, and glorified God.

And the ruler of the synagogue answered with indignation, because that Jesus had healed on the sabbath day, and said unto the people, There are six days in which men ought to work: in them therefore come and be healed, and not on the sabbath day.

The Lord then answered him, and said, Thou hypocrite, doth not each one of you on the sabbath loose his ox or his ass from the stall, and lead him away to watering? And ought not this woman, being a daughter of Abraham, whom Satan hath bound, lo, these eighteen years, be loosed from this bond on the sabbath day? And when he had said these things, all his adversaries were ashamed: and all the people rejoiced for all the glorious things that were done by him.

Questions:

- Where was Jesus?
- Where was the woman?
- What was the woman doing there?

- What did Jesus call the woman?
- How was the woman afflicted?
- What does it say she had for 18 years?
- What was the reaction of the leader of the synagogue?
- What was the reaction of the people?

On the Sabbath, the congregation met in the synagogue. Jesus sees the woman, whom the Scripture states has a spirit of infirmity. The demon causes her body to be bowed down. Today, we would say "Osteoporosis." The Scripture does not say by whom or when the woman was diagnosed with a demon. Jesus cast out the demon and the woman was healed instantly.

The religious, legalistic demons of the synagogue leader made him object to the ministry. "Don't do it here, don't do it today." The woman, who was a woman of God, praised the Lord for her healing/deliverance. Nobody had to tell her to do it. (Today, at the conclusion of a deliverance session, I have to make the person praise and thank God.) And the congregation rejoiced, and they called the deliverance of the woman a "glorious thing."

It is important to note that Jesus said if it is okay to untie your animal and take him to water (on a Sabbath), why is it not okay to untie this woman, who is a daughter of Abraham?

Most important, notice (again) that Jesus declared that even though the woman was a daughter of Abraham, Satan had her bound for 18 years.

Conclusions:

- A son or daughter of Abraham can be bound by Satan.

- Religious and legalistic demons are opposed to deliverance.
- A sanctuary is as good a place to cast out demons as a home, street, sidewalk, countryside, seaside or graveyard.
- The people of God rejoice when they see someone being set free.

Study 13: Manifestations

Mark 9:14-27

And when he came to his disciples, he saw a great multitude about them, and the scribes questioning with them. And straightway all the people, when they beheld him, were greatly amazed, and running to him saluted him.

And he asked the scribes, What question ye with them? And one of the multitude answered and said, Master, I have brought unto thee my son, which hath a dumb spirit; And wheresoever he taketh him, he teareth him: and he foameth, and gnasheth with his teeth, and pineth away: and I spake to thy disciples that they should cast him out; and they could not.

He answereth him, and saith, O faithless generation, how long shall I be with you? how long shall I suffer you? bring him unto me. And they brought him unto him: and when he saw him, straightway the spirit tare him; and he fell on the ground, and wallowed foaming.

And he asked his father, How long is it ago since this came unto him? And he said, Of a child.

And ofttimes it hath cast him into the fire, and into the waters, to destroy him: but if thou canst do any thing, have compassion on us, and help us. Jesus said unto him, If thou canst believe, all things are possible to him that believeth. And straightway the father of the child cried out, and said with tears, Lord, I believe; help thou mine unbelief.

When Jesus saw that the people came running together, he rebuked the foul spirit, saying unto him, Thou dumb and deaf spirit, I charge thee, come out of him, and enter no more into him. And the spirit cried, and rent him sore, and came out of him: and he was as one dead; insomuch that many said, He is dead. But Jesus took him by the hand, and lifted him up; and he arose.

Questions:

- Where was Jesus when this happened?
- Was Jesus expecting the disciples to cast out the demon?
- Was this a private ministry?
- Was there a manifestation of the demon?
- Did Jesus command the demon to stop manifesting?
- Did the demon talk?
- Did Jesus investigate the cause (or legal right) of the demon?
- Did Jesus try to stop the demon from screaming and renting the boy?
- Was this an instant deliverance?

Jesus came down from the mountain where He was transfigured before three of His disciples, and when He reached the other nine disciples, there was a multitude around them including some scribes who were questioning the nine.

A man came to Him and explained that he had brought his son who had a dumb spirit. Notice that the man already knew that the son had a dumb spirit. Again, I say in those times, most everyone knew about demons, and most everyone could tell when a person had a demon.

The disciples could not cast the demon out, and they brought the boy to Jesus. When the boy (or rather, the demon in the boy) saw Jesus, the demon started manifesting. The demon tore the boy, threw him to the ground and made him convulse and foam at the mouth. This seems very similar to an episode of epilepsy, which is what we would say today.

Notice that Jesus was not impressed by the manifestation, nor did He try to stop it. Neither was He concerned that the people might be frightened. Some pastors and ministers today don't want the demon to manifest, and they shout to the demon to stop manifesting. I often wonder what the reason for this is. Self-righteousness? Fear in the congregation? Fear in the pastor?

Perhaps as a lesson for the disciples, Jesus looked for the legal rights that the demon had to be in the boy. He asked the father how long the demon had been in the boy. The father said since childhood, which denoted an inherited demon, which probably entered the family because of sin or through a curse. A conversation about the unbelief of the father ensued, because this was also giving additional rights to the demon. During all this time, the demon continued manifesting.

Upon seeing the people approaching, Jesus commanded the dumb and deaf demon to go. The demon did not go instantly; more manifestations took place before the demon finally left.

Conclusions:

- Jesus ministered in the open countryside.
- There was a multitude watching.
- He expected His disciples to cast the demon out.
- The father of the boy knew a demon and not a sickness was in the boy.
- The demon manifested violently.
- Jesus let the demon manifest.
- Jesus researched the reason for the demon entering the boy.
- Jesus commanded the demon out, but the demon continued manifesting before coming out.
- It was not an instant deliverance.
- Jesus allowed the manifestations to happen.

How Did The Lord Minister Deliverance?

Exactly the opposite of what the criticisms, objections and roadblocks to deliverance are today.

- Where did He minister? Anywhere there was a demon! In sanctuaries, in homes, in the street, in the countryside, by the seashore, in a graveyard.

- Did He let the demons talk? And scream? He did! And He talked to them also! The only time He shut them up was when they said that He was the Son of God.

- Did He "approve" of manifestations? He certainly did. Manifestations were not an issue with Jesus!

- Did He only do "private" ministry? Not at all! The synagogues He ministered in were full of congregants who watched everything and magnified God for what Jesus did. He ministered at a home

> because He went to the sick woman in bed. He ministered on the sidewalk in front of the same home with many people watching. He ministered outdoors in the open under the clear blue skies with multitudes watching. He even ministered in a graveyard!

If Jesus came to your church service next Sunday, incognito, dressed in a sports shirt and denim pants, penny loafers with no socks, His hair in a pony tail, and started commanding a demon out of someone, what would your pastor say? What would YOU think?

Concerns

Even if Jesus ministered deliverance the way we have studied above, we must remember that in a situation such as a church, there is a chain of authority that must be respected. No one should go into a church and minister anything, much less deliverance, without the pastor's approval.

If you feel that you are called to a deliverance ministry, the first step is to receive deliverance yourself, and then learn all you can about it. The next step is to find an experienced deliverance minister and observe how he/she ministers. You can also attend the deliverance workshops at Hegewisch Baptist Church and Lake Hamilton Bible Camp.

If your church does not believe that Christians have demons, or your pastor does not want deliverance ministered in the church, and you feel that you are ready to minister deliverance (after receiving deliverance yourself), you need to find a church that believes that deliverance is for Christians, and stay there until the pastor allows you to minister. You can also go to "the highways and byways" to find the lost. Preach salvation, healing and deliverance, and minister to them.

Luke 14:16-24
Then said he unto him, A certain man made a great supper, and bade many: And sent his servant at supper time to say to them that were bidden, Come; for all things are now ready.

And they all with one consent began to make excuse. The first said unto him, I have bought a piece of ground, and I must needs go and see it: I pray thee have me excused. And another said, I have bought five yoke of oxen, and I go to prove them: I pray thee have me excused. And another said, I have married a wife, and therefore I cannot come.

So that servant came, and shewed his lord these things. Then the master of the house being angry said to his servant, Go out quickly into the streets and lanes of the city, and bring in hither the poor, and the maimed, and the halt, and the blind.

And the servant said, Lord, it is done as thou hast commanded, and yet there is room. And the lord said unto the servant, Go out into the highways and hedges, and compel them to come in, that my house may be filled. For I say unto you, That none of those men which were bidden shall taste of my supper.

Part 2

Legal Rights of Demons

Who gave Jacob for a spoil and Israel to the robbers? Did not the Lord, he against whom we have sinned? For they would not walk in his ways, neither were they obedient unto his law.

Isaiah 42:24

6 Legal Rights of Demons: Personal Sins

What Is a Legal Right?

Demons have legal rights to enter people. A legal right is what gives demons permission to enter someone. It is the reason for the entry of the demon. Sometimes it is called "opening the door to a demon"or "giving place to Satan." There are several reasons why demons may enter a person.

A demon that has a legal right to be in a person will be more difficult to cast out. When Jesus told someone, "Your sins are forgiven," He, in fact, destroyed the legal rights of the demons in that person, because He, the Son of God, forgave that person's sins.

When the legal right of the demon is destroyed, the demon does not leave of his own free will. To get the demon to leave, you have to cast it out in the name of Jesus.

This means, in representation of the Lord, as an ambassador or messenger.

Some people are afraid that if they are in the same room where the ministry of deliverance is taking place, the demons cast out are going to enter him/her. A demon does not enter a person just because he/she is hanging around in the room. Or next door. Or on the next block. A demon has to have a legal right to enter a person.

When a person gives a legal right to a demon, that demon is going to enter immediately. Not the next day and not the next year. Do not think that a demon entered you because it was cast out of another person, and that if you would not have been there, it would not have entered!

Known Legal Rights

I call the following "known legal rights" because they are the ones most deliverance ministers know about, so far.

1. Personal sins. Disobedience to God's commands gives legal rights to demons. You must know the Word of God, what He desires for us to do, and how He desires for us to behave. Most people have an idea of right and wrong, even when they have not read the Bible. Christians must go deeper than that. Christians need to keep the Word of God in their heart.

   Psalms 119:11
   Thy word have I hid in mine heart, that I might not sin against thee.

2. The sins of the fathers. These are the sins of our ancestors, and their punishment comes down through

the generations if they never repented. If our ancestors sinned and did not get right with God afterwards, the guilt of that sin is inherited, and the demons that had legal rights to enter our ancestors continue to have those legal rights in the following generations. See the second commandment. I know it does not sound fair, but it is the Word of God.

3. Curses placed on us. There are different sources of curses, and we will discuss them in a later chapter. A curse upon a person gives a demon a legal right to enter the person. The curse comes with a demon, and the demon works out the curse.

4. Curses placed on our ancestors. In the same way that the guilt of unrepented sins comes down the generations, curses come down the generations also because curses are inherited, giving legal rights to demons in each generation.

5. Evil things we have seen, heard or read. The impressions caused in our soul by evil and ugly things that we have seen with our eyes and heard with our ears give legal rights to demons for entering.

6. Consulting the occult. Since the occult arts or witchcraft are things the Lord hates, just the mere fact that you come near them, as in consulting a palm reader or a psychic, gives demons plenty of legal rights to enter. Even if you only accompanied someone to consult a psychic or fortune teller, you gave demons legal rights to enter you as well. Even if you don't believe in the supernatural, when you

enter occult territory, you open the doors to demons.

7. Practicing the occult. If consulting the occult gives legal rights to demons, imagine what practicing the occult does.

8. Owning accursed things. Owning things such as idols or objects used in pagan worship, drug paraphernalia, etc. gives legal rights to demons to enter the owner.

9. Owning objects with occult or pagan symbols. Objects such as jewelry, garments with symbols printed in the fabric, mugs, furniture, lamps, accessories, key rings, etc., give demons legal rights to enter buyers/owners of such things. The list is endless.

10. Evil Soul Ties. Evil soul ties we have with other people, animals or objects are a bridge for demons to enter.

11. Physical and emotional trauma. Trauma opens the doors to demons.

12. Satanic rituals/dedications. Having been dedicated as a child to other gods or to Satan by parents or grandparents opens big doors to demons.

The above reasons are discussed in detail in this chapter and in the following chapters.

Personal Sins

The following is a list of most common personal sins.

- Selfishness

- Rebellion
- Fear
- Unforgiveness
- Pride
- Lust
- Envy and Jealousy
- Greed

1- Selfishness

A selfish person is an egotist who is concerned chiefly or only with himself without regard for the well-being of others.

I have headed the above list of personal sins with "selfishness", because I believe it is the worst sin. In my 25 years of ministering deliverance I have discovered that selfish people have difficulty in being set free. It is not that they do not receive deliverance, but it is that they always have demonic problems. They are the ones who come to deliverance session after deliverance session, year after year, and yet they always need more deliverance.

Having ministered to several people who fit this description, I pondered their problem. I believe the Holy Spirit enlightened me about the common denominator they all had: selfishness. Surprised, I determined that they all had these common characteristics:

1. *Selfish people do not realize that they are selfish.* They are completely blind to that fact. They cannot recognize that they are selfish. Most people can recognize their sins, even if they do not admit them. Selfish people do not realize that they are selfish. If you confront a selfish person and tell him that he is

selfish, he will vehemently deny it.
This happened to me with one woman. She realized that she continued to be tormented by demons through the years, no matter how much deliverance she received. She complained to me about it and wanted me to come up with the answer. By that time, I knew the answer, and I also knew she would not accept my answer. She insisted so much that I finally told her, "Alright, you want to know why? You are selfish!" Her immediate response was, "I am NOT selfish!" She wanted to know why I was accusing her of being selfish. I told her certain things she had done that I considered selfish. She denied everything and got so angry with me that she never called me again.

2. *Selfish people only talk about themselves*. They may call you and ask, "How are you?" but they are really not interested in knowing. Some do not even ask. They call to talk about themselves. So after the social preliminaries, if any, they start their monologue of all kinds of details of their lives, their likes or dislikes, their discomforts, their sleep, their dreams and nightmares, what they ate (in detail), how they digested it, etc. It seems they do not have much else on their minds.

3. *When selfish people call, they do not even ask if you are busy or if you are free to talk to them*. They just start talking. They call because they need prayer from you, or they need to let off steam, or they need a phone number you have, or whatever their need is at the moment. When they do not need you, they do not call. If they are perfectly happy and in good

health, they do not call you. They do not call on your birthday. They do not call at Christmas. If they call, it is for something they need, not to wish you a nice day.

4. *When selfish people want something from you, they want it right away. If you do not drop what you are doing to attend to their need, they get offended.* Once, a woman started calling me regularly for prayer. In fact, she made me her "prayer partner" without consulting me about it first. She would call me at any time and immediately tell me, "We have to pray about this...." Several times she called when it was not convenient; nevertheless, I took time to pray with her. A few times, she called at dinner time. One evening, we were having dinner when the telephone rang, and my husband complained. I answered the phone and told her that we were having dinner and to please call back later. She answered in disbelief, "You cannot pray with me now?" I assured her that I could not, and she got angry with me and never called again.

5. *Selfish people have no regard for another person's time.* They are never on time for their appointments. They're on their own schedule, and you have to wait until they show up. If you agreed to meet them at a certain time, and they're late, it's most likely because something (non-critical) diverted their attention away from their commitment to be there on time, such as an interesting TV show or a garage sale they passed by on the way to see you. They know you are waiting, but they don't care, because in their minds they are #1. They are overtly or unconsciously of

> the opinion that your time is not as valuable as theirs. People who care about other people do not make them wait!

Selfishness sometimes goes with control. When a selfish person calls me for deliverance, sometimes there is a struggle about the time and place. They want the time and place that are convenient for them. Sometimes they say, "Oh, that is really so far away from me! Why don't you come here?" They also are not willing to cancel appointments and change their schedule, because they want me to cancel my appointments and change my schedule to accommodate theirs.

Once, I was in a small church for two years. I tried to introduce deliverance - the pastor had told me that it was needed - but few people were interested. At that time I thought I should be in the ministry full-time, but having realized I was wrong, I took a full-time job. One morning at work, I got a call from a couple from the church that I had left by that time. They had not been interested in learning about deliverance while I was in that church, but now they had a relative who needed deliverance urgently. The relative lived out of town, so they wanted to come by my office and pick me up immediately without allowing me to go home and pack a bag! I explained that I had a job and could not leave for several days just like that. I suggested that they take their pastor. They were offended and never called me back.

I hope that these examples of selfishness I have given serve as a checklist. I would like for you, my Christian brothers and sisters, to examine yourselves and see if your behavior fits the descriptions written above. **Because as long as you are selfish, it will be difficult for you to be completely free.**

A selfish person needs deliverance over and over again!

What the Scriptures Say About Selfishness

There are several Scriptures that agree about selfishness. You will understand the gravity of this sin from the following Scriptures:

Matthew 22:35-40
Then one of them, which was a lawyer, asked him a question, tempting him, and saying, Master, which is the great commandment in the law? Jesus said unto him, Thou shalt love the Lord thy God with all thy heart, and with all thy soul, and with all thy mind. This is the first and great commandment. And the second is like unto it, Thou shalt love thy neighbour as thyself. On these two commandments hang all the law and the prophets.

The word "hang" is the Greek word #2910 of the *Strong's Concordance*. It means just that, "hang." From *Webster's Dictionary*, I have taken the two most appropriate definitions.

1- <u>To attach to something above with no support from below</u>.

I envision a spiritual structure where the most important is above (love God with all your heart, love your neighbor as yourself), and what follows below is connected and attached to that. If the structure above did not exist or was not be strong enough, the hanging structure (what the law requires and what the prophets taught) would fall. In other words, if you are strongly religious and comply with all the requirements of the law and all that the prophets taught, but you do not love God or your neighbors, you are hanging onto nothing.

2- The underlying thought, main thread, drift.

The underlying thought, main thread and drift of Christianity is to love God with all your heart and to love your neighbor as yourself. The Lord has shown me that when we love Him intensely, His love is poured down on us in such a way that it overflows, and we cannot help but love others. The bottom line is, selfish people, because they only love themselves and not others, don't really love God.

Matthew 7:12
Therefore all things whatsoever ye would that men should do to you, do ye even so to them: for this is the law and the prophets.

There is a spiritual law here: you will be treated the same way that you treat others. This law is the same as, *"Give, and it shall be given unto you..."*.

Galatians 5:14
For all the law is fulfilled in one word, even in this; Thou shalt love thy neighbour as thyself.

Romans 13:9
For this, Thou shalt not commit adultery, Thou shalt not kill, Thou shalt not steal, Thou shalt not bear false witness, Thou shalt not covet; and if there be any other commandment, it is briefly comprehended in this saying, namely, Thou shalt love thy neighbour as thyself.

James 2:8
If ye fulfil the royal law according to the Scripture, Thou shalt love thy neighbour as thyself, ye do well.

Selfish Christian, after all these Scriptures, all I can say is: Repent! And you will enjoy lasting deliverance.

2 - Rebellion

We know that rebellion is not complying with the rules of the authority that is over us. Rebellion can be against our spiritual authority, God, or earthly authorities. Rebellion against earthly authorities includes rebellion against parents, teachers, the laws of the country, traffic laws, immigration laws, the boss, the supervisor, etc.

Rebellion Against God

Rebellion against God includes idolatry, witchcraft, and the occult. These activities carry a price to pay in the spiritual realm, even if you are active in them because of ignorance. The occult and witchcraft will be discussed in another chapter.

Idolatry and Abominations

Idolatry is anything that comes between you and God because you esteem it more important than God. A person may idolize his/her spouse, child, an animal, a hobby, a sport, a sports figure, a show business performer, or a vice. If you can't go to church because you have to play golf, or if you leave church early because of a football game, you are idolizing a sport. You idolize money, jewelry or a car, if your thoughts are about these things more than about God. Some people idolize their careers or their jobs. Some idolize their computers. Some people neglect not only God, but also their spouse and children because of idolatries.

Through my personal experience, I discovered that there is another type of idolatry that is described in the Bible clearly. However, during all my time in church, I never heard any teaching about this kind of idolatry:

Exodus 20:3-5

Thou shalt have no other gods before me. Thou shalt not make unto thee any graven image, or any likeness of any thing that is in heaven above, or that is in the earth beneath, or that is in the water under the earth. Thou shalt not bow down thyself to them, nor serve them: for I the Lord thy God am a jealous God, visiting the iniquity of the fathers upon the children unto the third and fourth generation of them that hate me;

Deuteronomy 4:15-20

Take ye therefore good heed unto yourselves; for ye saw no manner of similitude on the day that the Lord spake unto you in Horeb out of the midst of the fire: Lest ye corrupt yourselves, and make you a graven image, the similitude of any figure, the likeness of male or female, The likeness of any beast that is on the earth, the likeness of any winged fowl that flieth in the air, The likeness of any thing that creepeth on the ground, the likeness of any fish that is in the waters beneath the earth:

And lest thou lift up thine eyes unto heaven, and when thou seest the sun, and the moon, and the stars, even all the host of heaven, shouldest be driven to worship them, and serve them, which the Lord thy God hath divided unto all nations under the whole heaven. But the Lord hath taken you, and brought you forth out of the iron furnace, even out of Egypt, to be unto him a people of inheritance, as ye are this day.

Deuteronomy 7:25-26

The graven images of their gods shall ye burn with fire: thou shalt not desire the silver or gold that is on them, nor take it unto thee, lest thou be snared therein: for it is an abomination to the Lord thy God. Neither shalt thou bring an abomination into thine house, lest thou be a cursed thing like it: but thou shalt utterly detest it, and thou shalt utterly abhor it; for it is a cursed thing.

Study well and analyze the Scriptures above. They say to you not to make (or have) images of men or women, or of animals that fly in the air, that walk on earth or that swim in the water. Do not worship sun, moon or stars. This probably also meant not to have images of them.

The first two Scriptures above are the second commandment of the ten given to Moses on the mountain, written with the finger of God in stone. If God put them in the order that He wanted, then this commandment is more important than not taking the name of the Lord in vain, not murdering, not stealing. . . it is a very important commandment! This commandment is for today, just the same as it was in Old Testament times. Jesus is the same yesterday, today and forever. God does not change (*Hebrews 13:8*).

Before you make a decision in your heart about what I am saying here, please pray and seek the Lord about it. If you feel strong opposition to this, ask The Holy Spirit to guide you. Remember that Jesus did not come to destroy the law, but to fulfill it.

Some people think it is okay to have a statue or image in their home or at their work because they do not recognize it as the representation of another god or goddess. Perhaps you have a statue or painting and you know it is another god, such as Buddha, but you think that God won't mind it because you are not worshiping it or praying to it. You reason, "I am a good Christian, I read my Bible all the time, I pray to my God only, I go to church every time it is open." In fact, you have those objects only for decorative purposes and nothing else. Right? Wrong!

Wrong! How wrong I was! I was a baby Christian, and

that was exactly my line of thinking every time the Holy Spirit would tell me, *"Why do you have this statue here?"* Or, *"Why do you have this idol here?"* I would tell the Holy Spirit the same reasoning I wrote above, because I really did not know that the object I had was an idol. I told Him I was not worshiping it. But God is a jealous God! My argument was overruled. If God loves you, then He wants you as far from an idol or image as the east is from the west, because He is very jealous. And in spite of His love, there is a price to pay if you do have an idol or image in your house. Spiritual laws are continuously at work!

Even with the prompting of the Holy Spirit, I did not get rid of the abominations I had, because I thought there was no harm in them. The time came when the Lord wanted me to have deliverance. I heard Him say, "You have demons, and you need to have them cast out." He helped me find the best place to have deliverance ministered to me. Among all the demons from which I was delivered, I discovered that I had a demon that had come from one of the items in question. I know it because the Lord gave the woman who was ministering to me a vision of the exact item. She described it perfectly. Then she had a word of knowledge about another item, which was an image. Later I had deliverance from a werewolf demon, which entered me because I owned an American Indian image.

If you would like to know more about my testimony of this deliverance of idolatry, please order booklet #39, *Idols and Images,* from WRW Publications.

As a commercial interior designer at that time. I can tell you that when I went to showrooms, I could discern demons in many, many items. Be careful of what you bring into your home! We are very ignorant of the gods of other religions, their religious artifacts, their symbols and their witchcraft. We can easily bring what is an abomination to our God into our home and not know it. If you travel a lot, be careful what you bring home. If you do not know what a figure or symbol represents, do not buy it or acquire it. Do not bring home anything from lands that have another god or gods, or at least break the curses on them (before you buy them, if possible). Even here in the U.S., be careful when you buy anything made by people who worship other gods.

Dolls

A doll is a representation of a human figure. Look up the word doll in your dictionary or encyclopedia. Most of them say that dolls have their origin in witchcraft, and they are still used in witchcraft.

There are documented testimonies of people (adults and children) who have had strange supernatural experiences with dolls. I have read testimonies of people who have seen dolls dancing, and a testimony of a couple who were doll collectors who began attending Hegewisch Church. When they heard the teaching about dolls, they decided to get rid of the doll collection that they had in their attic. When they went to the attic, they heard doll voices telling them not to throw them away!

If you try to reason this out, it will impossible without the Holy Spirit. Let the Holy Spirit guide you about this. Seek God about it. We cannot fully understand the laws and ways of God and the spiritual world with our intellect. We can only understand them with our spirit. His thoughts are higher than our thoughts, and His ways are higher than our ways. We can use all our education, intellect, mind, sophistication and experience, but it will never reach God's knowledge. And when he puts bits of His knowledge in us, we may be blocking them out with our intellect. This is the war between our flesh and our spirit. Keep an open mind and an open ear to what the Lord might tell you.

The Cleansing of Our Homes

Children have very acute discernment of spirits. Adults, who lost this discernment long ago, think that their children's imaginations are working overtime. But when a child says, "There is a monster under my bed," it is most probable that there is a demon lurking in the darkness.

The first step in cleaning your house is to get rid of all statues, images, kachina dolls, books dealing with the occult and new age, drug paraphernalia, stuffed animals, dolls, jewelry or clothing with symbols, etc. The best thing to do is to ask the Holy Spirit to show you the things that you need to get rid of.

Take those things outside. Repent and ask the Father to forgive you for having bought them or received them into your home. Burn everything that can be burned and destroy those items that cannot be burned, rebuking them in the name of Jesus. Do not sell or give away any of those items, and do not put them in the garbage can without burning or destroying them. Make a list of the things you disposed of, because you will need deliverance of the demons that entered with each of those things.

Deuteronomy 7:25-26
The graven images of their gods shall ye burn with fire: thou shalt not desire the silver or gold that is on them, nor take it unto thee, lest thou be snared therein: for it is an abomination to the Lord thy God. Neither shalt thou bring an abomination into thine house, lest thou be a cursed thing like it: but thou shalt utterly detest it, and thou shalt utterly

abhor it; for it is a cursed thing.

Expelling Demons From Your Home

There are two misconceptions that I want to set right about cleansing your home from demons. First, I have found many times that homeowners anoint doors and windows in the belief that somehow that will get the demons out. This is based on the Passover story (Exodus 12). I do not know who started this teaching, but it is very popular although erroneous. If you read Exodus 12, you will find that the blood of the lamb was put on the door lintel and jambs to signal the angel of Death not to enter that house.

In the case of the demons inside your home being cast out, if you think that anointing oil around the windows and doors is going to prevent them from coming in, then it will also prevent them from going out! In reality the demons do not need doors and windows to go in and out of a house. And if you anoint, but do not command them out, they will not leave. Beware: if you bring an abomination into your house after you have anointed and commanded the demons out of your house, they will be back.

Secondly, do not use store-bought anointing oil. It does not have special powers or special anointing. Besides, there is a curse upon whoever mixes anointing oil according to the recipe of the Bible and also upon whoever uses it. If you are a child of God and walking straight before Him, this is what you do: pray over a small cup of fresh olive oil (about two tablespoons), and it will be as anointed as if Billy Graham or Benny Hinn had prayed for it!

How to Go About It

Just pray over the oil to the Father, telling Him what

you want to do with it, and asking Him to put His Holy Spirit in it and make it a powerful oil to expel demons from your house. Then, go to the places where you had the abominations and all the dark places of the house, dip your finger in the oil and touch the wall or behind the cabinet, etc. and command the demons there to leave in the name of Jesus and never to come back.

The dark places of the house are the places where the light does not shine or rarely shines: closets, inside cabinet doors and drawers, behind furniture, under furniture, etc.

Demons in Objects

You might have been taught that inanimate objects do not have demons, which is not correct teaching (see the Chippendale chairs story in Chapter 2). Some objects do have demons, and it does not matter if the demons are inside or sitting on the object. You don't want those demons in your house anyway. I am not talking about idols, images or things with questionable symbols on them. Those, you burn. I am talking about regular, everyday objects.

3 - Fear

Fear does not seem to be a sin, right? Nobody goes to jail for being fearful! So, why bring it up? In the eyes of God, fear is a sin because at its root is lack of trust in God. It is the opposite of trusting God. There are plenty of Scriptures telling us not to fear and to trust God, and when the theme of a Scripture is repeated throughout the Bible as it is with fear, we need to pay attention to it. In the book of Revelation, there is a list which shows the people who are going to Hell. Guess who heads the list? The fearful!

Revelation 21:7-8
He that overcometh shall inherit all things; and I will be his God, and he shall be my son. But the fearful, and unbelieving, and abominable, and murderers, and whoremongers, and sorcerers, and idolaters, and all liars, shall have their part in the lake which burneth with fire and brimstone: which is the second death.

The fearful go to Hell before murderers, witches and idolaters. Watch out, liars are last on the list, but are still going to the same place.

The fearful do not have faith and are really not believers. Any little fear opens the door to demons of fear, and these open the door to terror, and finally paranoia. The Word of God insists that we be courageous.

In the book of Job, we see that God gave permission to Satan to bother Job. Among all of Job's righteousness, there was a little flaw. A Scripture reveals it, but it is easily missed:

Job 3:25
For the thing which I greatly feared is come upon me, and that which I was afraid of is come unto me.

Job was fearful. It might have been Job's only sin. But fear is a "big" sin in the eyes of God. And the Lord wants His people to be delivered from the demons of fear. If you are fearful or have any specific kind of fear, try to overcome it yourself.

When I was a little girl, I was afraid of the dark. To comply with a promise I made to my Dad, I tried to overcome it. When the Lord saw that I was battling it, He supernaturally delivered me from demons of fear in a spectacular way. I believe that if I had not tried valiantly to overcome fear, I would have not been delivered.

Study the following Scriptures very carefully. They might speak to you in a personal way. Possess your Promised Land!

Deuteronomy 1:21

Behold, the Lord thy God hath set the land before thee: go up and possess it, as the Lord God of thy fathers hath said unto thee; fear not, neither be discouraged.

Joshua 1:9

Have not I commanded thee? Be strong and of a good courage; be not afraid, neither be thou dismayed: for the Lord thy God is with thee whithersoever thou goest.

Joshua 8:1

And the Lord said unto Joshua, Fear not, neither be thou dismayed: take all the people of war with thee, and arise, go up to Ai: see, I have given into thy hand the king of Ai, and his people, and his city, and his land:

Isaiah 41:10

Fear thou not; for I am with thee: be not dismayed; for I am thy God: I will strengthen thee; yea, I will help thee; yea, I will uphold thee with the right hand of my righteousness.

Numbers 14:9

Only rebel not ye against the Lord, neither fear ye the people of the land; for they are bread for us: their defence is departed from them, and the Lord is with us: fear them not.

John 14:27

Peace I leave with you, my peace I give unto you: not as the world giveth, give I unto you. Let not your heart be troubled, neither let it be afraid.

Ezekiel 2:6
And thou, son of man, be not afraid of them, neither be afraid of their words, though briers and thorns be with thee, and thou dost dwell among scorpions: be not afraid of their words, nor be dismayed at their looks, though they be a rebellious house.

Isaiah 8:12-13
Say ye not, A confederacy, to all them to whom this people shall say, A confederacy; neither fear ye their fear, nor be afraid. Sanctify the Lord of hosts himself; and let him be your fear, and let him be your dread.
To be courageous is God's command, not a suggestion.

4 - Unforgiveness

To hold a grudge against a person is the opposite of forgiving. God said we have to forgive, so if you do not forgive, you sin. Unforgiveness and resentment open the door to diseases such as cancer and arthritis. This has been well known not only in deliverance ministries but also in healing ministries. Lately, the medical field has also been investigating this.

There is a need to forgive because, if we do not forgive, God will not forgive us. When the disciples told Jesus, "Lord, teach us to pray," He taught them as an example the prayer we now call "The Lord's Prayer". It includes, "... *and forgive us our debts as we also have forgiven our debtors,"* (Matthew 6:12). This Scripture is telling us:

- If we forgive, God forgives us.

- In the same measure we forgive, God forgives us

(happily, grudgingly, half-way, etc.).

- If we do not forgive, God does not forgive us.

Mark 11:25-26
And when ye stand praying, forgive, if ye have ought against any: that your Father also which is in heaven may forgive you your trespasses. But if ye do not forgive, neither will your Father which is in heaven forgive your trespasses.

Matthew 6:14-15
For if ye forgive men their trespasses, your heavenly Father will also forgive you: But if ye forgive not men their trespasses, neither will your Father forgive your trespasses.

Demons Enter When You Do Not Forgive

Demons have a legal right to enter a person who does not forgive. The reason that God wants you to forgive is that forgiving helps you more than it helps the offending party. If you forgive, you get the benefit of forgiving, but if you don't and keep your bitterness and resentment, you will open the door to the demons of unforgiveness, resentment, rancor, hate and even murder. Then diseases set in, even when God wants us healthy. It is the will of God that we be healthy, and this is why He commands us to forgive.

Matthew 18:32-35
Then his lord, after that he had called him, said unto him, O thou wicked servant, I forgave thee all that debt, because thou desiredst me: Shouldest not thou also have had compassion on thy fellowservant, even as I had pity on thee?

And his lord was wroth, <u>and delivered him to the tormentors,</u> till he should pay all that was due unto him. So likewise shall my heavenly Father do also unto you, if ye from your hearts forgive not every one his brother their trespasses.

Who are the tormentors? They are the demons mentioned above. If you want to receive deliverance, you need to forgive everyone that "owes" you something, even if they are already dead. All of us have someone to forgive: parents, teachers, relatives, pastors, husbands, wives, friends, doctors, lawyers, neighbors, murderers, rapists. Don't forget to forgive God also, if you have blamed Him for anything. And finally, forgive yourself!

Forgive, No Matter What

God wants you to forgive regardless of the kind of offense or even crime that was committed against you. It does not matter if the person who hurt you was extremely wrong, and you were extremely right. You have to truly forgive. You have to loose rancor from your heart, and let it go. Think of it this way: He cannot judge that person until you forgive him/her, and your forgiving releases that person into God's hands for judging.

Romans 12:19
Dearly beloved, avenge not yourselves, but rather give place unto wrath, for it is written: "Vengeance is mine, I will repay, says the Lord."

Matthew 18:21-22
Then came Peter to him, and said, Lord, how oft shall my brother sin against me, and I forgive him? till seven times? Jesus saith unto him, I say not unto thee, Until seven times: but, Until seventy times seven.

Forgiving And Forgetting

Some people are still too emotional and too hurt when the time comes for forgiving. The minister needs to ask the person, "Are you willing to forgive, even if it hurts?" If the person says yes, then ask the person to forgive out of their will, and not out of their emotions. The will to forgive is good enough for the Lord. The person should pray that the Lord helps him/her to forgive. Then forgive the offending parties aloud, and ask God to forgive them also. The person should also ask God to forgive himself/herself.

Forgiving does not mean that you have to socialize with that person again. As for a relative, you must treat him/her as you would any other relative. If it was a friend, and the possibility exists that the friend may hurt you again, then do not renew the friendship. This does not mean you have not forgiven. It means you are protecting yourself and setting boundaries.

Forgiving also does not mean forgetting. If you happen to remember the incident, it does not mean that you have not forgiven. After you forgive, the memory will not hurt you as much as it did before, or not at all.

5 - Pride

Pride is what caused Lucifer, the cherub who covered the throne of God, to be thrown down from heaven. Pride means to think highly of yourself, which makes you think that everyone else is inferior to you. A person may feel proud because of race, nationality, beauty, money, education, family name, success in the business world, etc. The ugliest of all the forms of pride is religious pride, because it sometimes hurts tender baby Christians.

Sometimes, pride is subtle. It may not be blatant or show up in arrogance, but it may show up in subtle ways. If you have a friend who is trying to help you by "fixing' things that she perceives are wrong with you, it is pride disguised as helpfulness. Your friend thinks that you are not good enough, but thinks that she is, so she feels she can teach you and perfect you.

The opposite of pride is meekness and humility. Jesus, the Son of God, the King of Kings and Lord of Lords, said he was meek:

Matthew 11:29
Take my yoke upon you, and learn of me: for I am meek and lowly of heart, and you shall find rest unto your souls.

If Jesus, King of Kings and Lord of Lords is meek, who are we to be proud?

Promises for the Meek

In the Word of God, there are many promises for the meek and humble:

Matthew 5:5
Blessed are the meek: for they shall inherit the earth.

Matthew 18:4
Whosoever therefore shall humble himself as this little child, the same is greatest in the kingdom of heaven.

Matthew 23:12
And whosoever shall exalt himself shall be abased; and he that shall humble himself shall be exalted.

James 4:6
But he giveth more grace. Wherefore he saith, God resisteth the proud, but giveth grace unto the humble.

7 Legal Rights of Demons: The Sins of the Fathers

The "sins of the fathers," as the Word of God calls them, are also called generational sins or generational curses. I call them the sins of the fathers, because this is what the Bible calls them.

When our ancestors sinned, they opened doors for demons to come into them. These demons have legal rights to stay in the families, so they come down through the generations. Some demons show up in every generation, and some skip one generation. These demons are inherited, and they may enter even at the time of conception. Are you in sin? Your children, grandchildren and following generations will inherit the demons that you are allowing to enter today!

Exodus 20:4-5
Thou shalt not make unto thee any graven image, or any likeness of any thing that is in the heavens above, or that is

in the earth beneath, or that is in the water under the earth. Thou shalt not bow down thyself to them, nor serve them: for I the Lord thy God am a jealous God, visiting the iniquity of the fathers upon the children unto the third and fourth generation of them that hate me.

The above Scripture is the second of the Ten Commandments. The second commandment instructs us not to make or have any images of man or woman, or of any animals that walk or slide on the ground, that fly in the air or that swim in the water. Furthermore, it says not to worship them. This commandment also says that God "visits" the iniquity of the fathers upon the children to the third and fourth generation. (For more on this commandment, see Deuteronomy 5:8, 9.)

The word "visit" is the Hebrew word #6485 of *Strong's Concordance*, and it means *avenge* and *punish.*

Although the Lord saw fit to explain that He visits the sins of the fathers upon the children in this particular commandment, it is not only on the breaking of the second commandment that He avenges the sins of the fathers. He punishes any kind of sin of the ancestors in the following generations, and the type of punishment is related to the kind of sin committed.

Exodus 34:6-7

And the Lord passed by before him, and proclaimed: The Lord, the Lord God, merciful and gracious, longsuffering and abundant in goodness and truth. Keeping mercy for thousands, forgiving iniquity and transgression and sin, and that will by no means clear the guilty: visiting the iniquity of the fathers upon the children's children, unto the third and to the fourth generation.

Hosea 4:6

My people are destroyed for lack of knowledge; because thou hast rejected knowledge, I will also reject thee, that thou shalt be no priest to me: seeing thou hast forgotten the law of thy God, I will also forget thy children.

In my 25 years of experience in the deliverance ministry, I have discovered that inherited demons do not leave after the fourth generation. No demons leave by their own volition. They have to be cast out.

Have you ever said that a particular habit or personality trait "runs in the family"? Maybe you have heard someone say that "stubbornness runs in the family," or "impatience runs in the family." What is running in the family is an inherited demon! Also, diseases that run in the family are provoked by inherited demons.

I have heard families comment on the antics of an ancestor, laughing and boasting over the actions of a deceased relative, whether it was moving fences to acquire more land, or stealing cattle, etc. The families are proud of what their ancestors did, because they inherited their money which was accumulated through trickery. Little do they know that the problems they may be experiencing today are directly related to those sins. If your ancestors did not keep "just balances" in their business deals, this could be the reason that you cannot find a job, or that you are not prosperous today. Prosperity has to do with much more than "naming it and claiming it"!

The first time I heard about the sins of the fathers was in 1980 at Hegewisch Baptist Church. At that time, no one else that I knew of was teaching about it. But because this church was one of the first, if not the first church devoted to setting the captives free, they were able to figure out that certain present-day problems that people were having were tied to the sins of their ancestors. If you would like more details, order booklet #24 from WRW Publications.

Through the ministry and practice of deliverance, many secrets of the kingdom are revealed. This is the Lord's reward for those who have the courage to face demons and cast them out.

How to Get Rid of Inherited Demons

As long as you are sincerely disdainful and remorseful of your ancestors' sins, you can follow these steps to receive your deliverance. Always remember that you are asking forgiveness for yourself, not for your ancestor.

1- If you know about your ancestors' sins, write them down. Do some research; ask your parents or grandparents who might tell you some stories. You might have heard stories in your family that actually described sinful behavior. On the other hand, if the family is ashamed of the sin, you may have never heard any stories. Find out where your ancestors lived and what their business was. Do not be afraid to ask point-blank about possible adultery, murder, witchcraft, etc. Do some research about the area they lived in and the customs and religion they had. Some families have had customs that were akin to witchcraft. For instance, when my grandmother had a long-winded visitor that overstayed the visit, my aunts would put a broom sprinkled with salt behind a door, believing that it would make the visitor leave. Now that I am a Christian and know about spiritual things, I realize that this was witchcraft, even if they did not know it or intended it to be so. I have discovered that Mexican-American families think that rubbing a raw egg on a sick child to cure him is not witchcraft. They just think it is a home remedy.

2- Prepare for confession and repentance. Have a frank talk with the Lord and admit to Him that what your ancestor did was a sin. Once you have confessed those actions as sins, repent. This means, repent for what your ancestors did, tell the Lord you are not in agreement with the behavior, that you despise what they did, and that you yourself will not engage in the same thing, ever. Your motivation here is true repentance, heart-felt repentance. If your motivation is getting rid of what ails you, and your repentance is faked, deliverance may not happen.

3- Ask the Lord for forgiveness for you. The forgiving is for you and your children, not for your ancestors. Many people whom I have helped go through this process wanted to ask forgiveness for the ancestors. It does not work that way.

4- Seek deliverance. Make a list of all you have discovered and bring your list with you to a deliverance minister who will break the inherited curses that might be in the family and cast out all the inherited demons that entered because of those curses.

The Old Testament's Confession and Repentance of the Sins of the Fathers

The Old Testament shows that the tribes of Israel were very much aware that their calamities were related to the sins of their ancestors, and they repented and prayed for forgiveness:

***2 Chronicles 29*:** Hezekiah, the king of Israel, did that which was right in the eyes of the Lord (verse 2). He realized that "our fathers have trespassed" (verse 6) and understood that what his country was going through was a consequence of that sin (verse 9) and was considering repentance (verse 10).

***2 Chronicles 30*: Hezekiah sends a letter appealing to the people to repent from the sins of their fathers (verses 6 to 9), but they laughed at him (verse 10). Nevertheless, some people agreed and came to Jerusalem to observe the Passover. Hezekiah prayed for them.

***Nehemiah*: Both the people of the kingdom of Judah and the kingdom of Israel had lost their land and gone into exile because of their disobedience to God. This disobedience had started generations before and now this generation was paying for it. After 70 years, the people of Israel were allowed to come back to the Promised Land with Ezra the prophet guiding them. Nehemiah, who was the king's cupbearer, did not go with the people but stayed at his job. One of his brothers came to visit him and told him that the walls of Jerusalem were broken, and the gates of the city burned with fire. Nehemiah grieved when he heard it. He prayed to God and confessed to Him, "Both I and my father's house have sinned," (chapter 1, verses 4-6).

Nehemiah went to Israel to repair the walls and the gates, and later Ezra gathered the people together and read them the law of the Lord, which they had never heard (chapter 8, verses 5-12). At the appropriate time, the people assembled to fast, mourn, repent, and confess their own sins and the sins of their fathers (chapter 9, verses 1 to 3, verse 16 and 17, 26 and 27).

Jeremiah 14:20-21

We acknowledge, O Lord, our wickedness, and the iniquity of our fathers: for we have sinned against thee, Do not abhor us, for thy name's sake, do not disgrace the throne of thy glory: remember, brake not thy covenant with us.

Jeremiah 16:11-13
Then shalt thou say unto them, Because your fathers have forsaken me, saith the Lord, and have walked after other gods, and have served them, and have worshipped them, and have forsaken me, and have not kept my law; And ye have done worse than your fathers; for, behold, ye walk everyone after the imagination of his evil heart, that they may not hearken unto me: Therefore will I cast you out of this land unto a land that ye know not, neither ye nor your fathers; and there shall you serve other gods day and night; where I will not shew ye favor.

Jeremiah 32:18
Thou showest loving kindness unto thousands, and recompensest the iniquity of the fathers into the bosom of their children after them: the Great, the Mighty God, the Lord of hosts, is his name.

Jeremiah 44:9
Have you forgotten the wickedness of your fathers, and the wickedness of the kings of Judah, and the wickedness of their wives, and your own wickedness, and the wickedness of your wives, which they have committed in the land of Judah, and in the streets of Jerusalem?

Lamentations 5:5-8
Our necks are under persecution: we labour and have no rest. We have given the hand to the Egyptians, and to the Assyrians, to be satisfied with bread. Our fathers have sinned, and are not; and we have borne their iniquities. Servants have ruled over us, there is none that doeth deliver us out of their hand.

Ezekiel 2:3
And he said unto me, Son of man, I send thee to the children of Israel, to a rebellious nation that hath rebelled against

me: they and their fathers have transgressed against me, even unto this very day.

Ezekiel 20:4
Wilt thou judge them, son of man, wilt thou judge them? Cause them to know the abominations of their fathers.

Ezekiel 20:27, 30
Therefore, son of man, speak unto the house of Israel , and say unto them, Thus saith the Lord God: yet in this your fathers have blasphemed me, in that they have committed a trespass against me, (30) Wherefore say unto the house of Israel, Thus saith the Lord God, Are you polluted after the manner of your fathers? And commit ye whoredom after the manner of their abominations?

The prophet Daniel prayed:

Daniel 9:16
O Lord, according to all thy righteousness, I beseech thee, let thy anger and thy fury be turned away from thy city Jerusalem, the holy mountain: because for our sins, and for the iniquities of or fathers, Jerusalem and thy people are become a reproach to all that are about us.

The prophet Zechariah prophesied:

Zechariah 1:2-5
The Lord hath been sore displeased with your fathers. Therefore say thou unto them, Thus saith the Lord of hosts; turn ye into me , saith the Lord of hosts, and I will turn into you, saith the Lord of hosts. Be ye not as your fathers, unto whom the former prophets have cried, saying, Thus saith the Lord of hosts, Turn ye now from your evil ways, and from your evil doings: but they did not hear, nor hearken unto

me, saith the Lord. Your fathers, where are they? And the prophets, do they live forever?

The "sins of the fathers" worksheet

How many ancestors do we have? Two parents, four grandparents, eight great-grandparents. Every generation back, the number doubles. Let's see how many ancestors we have counting to 20 generations back (get your calculator).

1st:2 2nd: 4 3rd: 8 4th:____ 5th:_____ 6th:______7th:_______

8th:_______9th:_______10th:________11th:________12th:_________

13th:____________14th:_____________15th:________________

16th:_____________17th:_____________18th:________________

19th:___________________20th:____________________________

Let's locate the 20th generation back in time: assume each generation as 25 years (people got married at a younger age before). 20 generations x 25 years per generation = 500 years

This year is:________ less 500 years makes it year:______________

We had ________________________ancestors in the year________

America had recently been discovered in that year. Your 20th generation ancestors were not American (unless you are 100% Native American). Where were your ancestors?_________________________________

What were they?____

What was their culture?__________________________________

Add up your ancestors (add up all the generations above)
____

Among that many people:

Do you think some may have worshiped other gods?_____________

Do you think some might have been witches or warlocks?________

Do you think some may have been thieves?____________________

Do you think some may have been pirates?____________________

Do you think some may have been adulterers?_________________

Do you think some may have been murderers?_________________

Do you think that some may have been child molesters?_________

Do you think some may have been pornographers?______________

Do you think some may have been blasphemers?_______________

Do you think some may have been any other kind of sinners?______

Or, perhaps, all of them were sinners?_______________________

Comments:

A demon is a curse and a curse always comes in with a demon. In other words, where there is a curse, there is a demon.

I mentioned before that ministers who are dedicated to deliverance, discover many things about the spiritual world and how it works. Many years ago deliverance ministers discovered that a curse and a demon come together.

I have noticed that things that are learned in the deliverance ministry trickle down to other ministries that may have nothing to do with deliverance. In fact, many of those ministries are entirely opposed to casting out demons. However, on Christian television I have heard ministers talk about the sins of the fathers, which they call generational curses, and about curses in general. They make a big deal about it (and it IS a big deal), but they fail to mention the most important thing: the demon that comes with the curse.

Of course, nobody wants to mention the "d" word. The only ones who use the word "demon" are deliverance ministers. And we are despised for using the "d" word so freely! Most ministers prefer to use the word "spirit" instead of the word "demon". The word demon means "evil spirit", not just spirit. Because God is a Spirit, I prefer to use the word demon when referring to evil spirits.

Not wanting to talk or teach about demons has consequences: people are kept in ignorance. Even the Word of God warns about ignorance of this kind:

Hosea 4:6

My people are destroyed for lack of knowledge: because thou hast rejected knowledge, I will also reject thee, that thou shalt not be a priest to me: seeing thou hast forgotten the law of thy God, I will also forget thy children.

Isaiah 5:13

Therefore, my people are gone into captivity, because they have no knowledge: and their honourable men are famished, and their multitude dried up with thirst.

Isaiah 28:9

Whom shall he teach knowledge? And whom shall he make to understand doctrine? Them that are weaned from the milk, and drawn from the breasts.

Hebrews 5:13-14:

For everyone that uses milk is unskillful in the word of righteousness: for he is a babe. But strong meat belongs to them that are full of age, even those who by reason of use have their senses exercised to discern both good and evil.

Break Curses, But Cast The Demon Out!

Any kind of curse can be broken in the name of Jesus, but you have to cast out the demon that came with it. When you break a curse, all you are doing is taking away the legal right that the demon had to be in the person. So, if this is all you do, the demon stays in the person. Because the demon came to work out the curse, if you don't cast it out, the demon continues to do his work.

Let's put it this way: a thief finds a house key. The key is his legal right to enter the house. He enters the house, but pretty soon the owner comes home and finds the thief. He takes away the key from the thief (taking away the thief's legal right) but does not kick the thief out of the house. The owner goes to bed. The thief stays, destroys and steals everything and might even murder the owner of the house.

This is what happens when a curse is broken but the demon is not cast out! The thief comes to destroy, steal and kill!

There Is More Than One Kind of Curse

There are different types of curses. The following is the way I categorize curses:

1. Biblical Curses

2. Witchcraft Curses

3. Charismatic Witchcraft Curses

4. Spoken Curses

5. Self-Curses

1 - Biblical Curses

There are many curses in the Word of God. These come as punishment upon people who do not obey God. Those curses are still in effect today. Some people believe that this concept is invalid, saying that because Jesus went to the cross and became a curse for us, now in New Testament times no curse can come upon us, much less Biblical curses.

In going to the cross, Jesus obtained many things for us, and I am sure that we do not know the half of it. But we know He obtained salvation for us: Is everyone saved? No. He obtained healing for us: Is everyone healed? No. Why? Because individually, each one of us has to appropriate those blessings, by confession, repentance, faith, etc. Jesus also obtained for us the power to break the Old Testament curses. In the same manner, now that we have the power to do it, each one of us must have the Biblical curses lifted by breaking them and casting out the demons that came with them.

I believe people in deliverance are prophetic people. We must hear from the Lord in order to be effective ministers. We might not be prophets, but we are prophetic. The Lord wants to set His people free, so He reveals to us what is needed to be done. I will be sharing with you many things that you may not have heard before. There are many curses in the Bible, and I will list some below, but by no means is this list comprehensive.

A) The Lord Reveals About the Curses of Poverty

Many years ago, I attended a Mexican-American church in Houston for a while. Several ladies of the church asked me to come to their homes to minister to their families. They lived in a certain neighborhood near the church.

When I went to these ladies' houses, I was shocked to see what I considered to be less than the dimensions necessary for adequate living rooms, bedrooms, etc. They could hardly place furniture in the rooms. These homes seemed like miniature houses to me.

Later, a pastor from Monterrey invited me to go to that city to teach deliverance. His church was in a very poor area, in a government "colonia". There I saw houses that were even smaller. This made me very unhappy, because these people were Christians, and they were living in houses that they could barely outfit with furniture.

During the next trip to that city, the pastor took me to a nearby town to preach in a church. On the way to the town, we met the pastor of the church. He told us that he was going to pray for an older female member of the congregation. We followed him down a dirt road. When we got to the woman's house, we saw that she lived in a big crate. Outside, she had a sort of barbecue pit where she could light a fire and cook her meals. She was not there at the time, because she was visiting her son at his house. When we arrived at the son's house, we found it to be a two-room house. He had built it of concrete block, but it still did not have windows or doors, only the openings for them.

When I came back home (my house then looked like a palace to me), I grieved for those people, and I kept asking myself, why are they so poor if they are God's children? What about the prosperity teaching that I had heard so often? In that small town, the pastor had taken us to his house, and he had sent for ice so that he could give us cold water to drink. This evidently was a luxury, because his children were jubilant at the thought of having ice water! It was not cake, or candy, or ice cream, but ice that made them joyful!

So, I asked the Lord to explain to me why they were so poor if they were His children. I did not hear anything right away. Two or three days later while driving to my office, I was listening to a tape. In the tape, a Scripture was mentioned, and then the Lord told me, "That's it! That's the reason for their poverty!"

When I got to my office, I started reading that Scripture, and the Lord said, "See, it is not one curse, but three that have to be broken." This is how I found out that Biblical curses have to be broken.

The Three Curses of Poverty

Genesis 3:17
And unto Adam he said, because thou hath hearkened unto the voice of thy wife, and hast eaten of the tree, of which I commanded thee saying, Thou shalt not eat of it: cursed is the ground for thy sake; in sorrow shalt thou eat of it all the days of thy life. (This is the curse of eating of the ground in sorrow.)

Genesis 3:18
Thorns also and thistles shalt it bring forth to thee; and thou shalt eat the herb of the field. (This is the curse of thorns and thistles.)

Genesis 3:19
In the sweat of thy face shalt thou eat bread, till thou return unto the ground; for out of it wast thou taken: for dust thou art, and unto dust shalt thou return. (This is the curse of eating in the sweat of our faces.)

These curses work this way: anything that can go wrong

will go wrong. These curses mean that you are not going to have a thing unless you work very hard for it, and work will become joyless. You will be looking ahead to the day when you retire! Everyone with whom you work will be hostile and hard to get along with, if not worse. Your boss will be hard to please. You will be in the rat race, even if you don't want to be in it. Anything that may go wrong with the development of your project will for sure go wrong. The people whom you hire will not help you and may stab you in the back. The equipment will break down and need to be replaced. You will not find important documents, because your secretary did not file them, etc. Does it sound familiar?

Earlier, in the agricultural society, these curses meant that weeds were going to grow and overtake what you planted; that the ground would be hard to work; that bugs would eat your plants; that it would not rain when you needed it, and it would rain too much when you did not need it. You would work in the field from sunup to sunset, and when you had one part of the field under control, another part would be sprouting weeds or infested with bugs.

Thanks be to Jesus that today we can break those curses and command the demons that came with them to leave us! Don't you like that? Only believe!

The Lord Reveals More Curses of Poverty

I was eager to start breaking these curses, so I called a friend over the phone and asked her if I could minister to her. She said yes, and she had a lot of deliverance from these curses. She invited some friends to come for the breaking of those curses. I ministered to her friends, and they had a lot of deliverance. The next time I broke those curses, the Lord told me, "Now go to Deuteronomy 28 and break those curses also." I did that immediately, and there was lots of deliverance from those curses. If you study these curses in detail, you will see that these curses pertain to different kinds of poverty, such as poverty of health, etc.

How to Break the Curses of Poverty

Breaking the three curses of Genesis and all the curses of Deuteronomy 28 takes a long time. This is why I prefer to break the curses as a mass or group deliverance of these curses rather than individually.

As all these curses come to us through the generations (all the way from Adam in the Genesis case), and the reason that they come upon us is because of disobedience. Repentance and asking forgiveness are needed (see chapter 7, *The Sins of the Fathers*).

After this is accomplished, start breaking the first curse in the name of Jesus, and cast out the demons that came with that curse. After ascertaining that all the demons came out, break the second curse in the name of Jesus and cast out all the demons that came with that curse. At each curse, take the time to cast out all the demons.

When I teach about breaking these curses of poverty, I find that some of my students want to lump everything together like this: "I break all the curses of Deuteronomy 28 in the name of Jesus." This is not the way the Lord told me to do it. They have to be broken and the demons cast out one by one.

As you break the last curse and cast out those demons, pray, if you feel led, that the Lord makes you a conduit of His blessings. Then, bless the people with the blessings of Deuteronomy 28. Don't forget to thank the Lord when you finish!

B) The Curse of Labor Pain

Genesis 3:16
Unto the woman he said, I will greatly multiply thy sorrow and thy conception; in sorrow thou shalt bring forth children; and thy desire shall be to thy husband, and he shall rule over thee.

C) The Curse of the Anointing Oil and the Incense

I feel certain that the anointing oil used by the early church was plain olive oil. I know that the apostles would not have dared mix and use the Levitical anointing oil. Why? Because it was an oil to be used only in the tabernacle, and later in the temple, to anoint the priests into service. It was exclusive, and it carried a curse for anyone who mixed it or used it for anything else.

This is a big surprise for many Christians who believe that the anointing oil they buy at the Christian bookstore is better than the olive oil they have in their kitchen pantry. The store-bought anointing oil clearly says that it has been compounded following the formula that is in the Bible. I wonder why Christian bookstores carry an anointing oil that the Bible specifically says not to replicate. Do the store owners read the Bible? Do the buyers of the oil read the Bible? If they do, do they believe what it says? Or do they just want to disobey? These are questions that I ask myself, because many times, when I get my oil to minister, someone runs to get the store-bought anointing oil to use instead.

Exodus 30:22-25, 31-33
Moreover, the Lord spake unto Moses, saying: Take thou also unto thee principal spices, of pure myrrh five hundred shekels, an of sweet cinnamon half so much, even two hundred

and fifty shekels, and of sweet calamus two hundred and fifty shekels, and of cassia five hundred shekels, after the shekel of the sanctuary, and of oil olive an hin: and thou shalt make it an oil of holy ointment, an ointment compound after the art of the apothecary: it shalt be an holy anointing oil....And thou shalt speak unto the children of Israel, saying, This shall be an holy anointing oil unto me throughout your generations, upon man's flesh shall it not be poured, neither shall ye make any other like it, after the composition of it: it is holy, and it shall be holy unto you. Whosoever compoundeth any like it, or whosoever putteth any of it upon a stranger, shall even be cut off from his people.

The incense of the tabernacle:

Exodus 30:34-35, 37-38
And the Lord said unto Moses, Take unto thee sweet spices, stacte, and onycha, and galbanum, these sweet spices with pure frankincense: of each shall there be like weight: and thou shalt make a perfume, a confection after the art of the apothecary, tempered together, pure and holy...And as for the perfume that thou shalt make, ye shalt not make for yourselves according to the composition thereof: it shall be unto thee holy for the Lord, whosoever shall make like unto that, to smell thereto, shall even be cut off from his people.

Disobedience to these two commands carries a curse of death.

D) The Curse Upon Idolaters

Exodus 20:4-5
Thou shalt not make unto thee any graven image, or any likeness of anything that is in heaven above, or that is in the earth beneath, or that is in the water under the earth: Thou shalt not bow down thyself to them, nor serve them: for I the

Lord thy God am a jealous God, visiting the iniquity of the fathers upon the children unto the third and fourth generation of them that hate me.

(This Scripture is the second commandment of the Ten Commandments.)

Exodus 22:20
He that sacrificeth unto any god, save unto the Lord only, he shall be utterly destroyed.

Deuteronomy 4:25-26
When thou shalt beget children, and children's children, and ye shall have remained long in the land, and shall corrupt yourselves, and make a graven image, or the likeness of anything, and shall do evil in the sight of the Lord thy God, to provoke him to anger: I call heaven and earth to witness against you this day, that you shall soon utterly perish from off the land whereunto ye go over to possess it; ye shall not prolong your days upon it, but shall utterly be destroyed.

The curse upon those who serve other gods, or possess images of other gods, whether they are sculptures or paintings of gods in the shape of persons or animals, is a curse of destruction.

E) Curse For Eating Fat

Leviticus 7:23-25
Speak unto the children of Israel, saying: ye shall eat no manner of fat, of ox, or of sheep, or of goat. And the fat of the beast that dieth of itself, and the fat of that which is torn with beasts, may be used in any other use: but ye shall in no wise eat of it. For whosoever eateth the fat of the beast, of which men offer an offering made by fire unto the Lord, even the soul that eateth it shall be cut off from his people.

F) Curse for Eating Blood

Leviticus 7:26-27

Moreover, ye shall eat no manner of blood, whether it be of fowl or of beast, in any of your dwellings. Whatsoever soul it be that eateth any manner of blood, even that soul shall be cut off from his people.

I have found that breaking the curses for eating fat and eating blood (and casting the demons out) is very effective in casting out a multitude of demons. Everyone should seek deliverance from these curses.

Please do not get upset about the following. I understand that this might be a paradigm shift for you. Please keep in mind that this book is about deliverance, and this section of the book is about things that opens doors to demons. It has nothing to do with salvation. We saw in the first chapter that your spirit is cleansed and sealed when you become a born-again Christian, and that now our goal is to rid our soul and body of evil spirits that have come in. In our quest for deliverance, we must be aware of the doors that have been open to the demons, in order to shut those doors and block the entrance of more of the same demons. The following might be shocking news to you. but please bear with me:

Just the same as eating blood open doors for the entrance of demons, I have found out that eating the foods prohibited in the dietary laws of Leviticus also opens doors for the entrance of demons. What happened is that as I would read those Scriptures, I could feel the Holy Spirit telling me not to eat those foods. Every time that I read them, I received the same impression. So I little by little I stopped eating them. Later the Holy Spirit impressed on me to do a deliverance of demons which entered through this door. As

I ministered to friends, we found out that demons did enter for eating pork, ham, bacon, shrimp, etc. Just remember this has nothing to do with your salvation. You do not go to hell for eating these foods. But you may get tormented with demons and, just as eating blood results in blood diseases, it is possible that eating these other foods result in digestive tract diseases.

I know about Peter's vision. Some of you might have experienced the Holy Spirit telling you the same that He was telling me. Some of you might agree with this, some might not. If you don't, first pray about it and ask the Lord if I am right or not. May the Lord guide you in this.

I understand that "the soul cut off from his people" means death; however, I do not think it is sudden death, but death through sickness and disease.

G) Curse for Drinking Wine or Alcohol Before Ministering

Leviticus 10:9
Do not drink wine nor strong drink, thou, nor thy sons with thee, when ye go into the tabernacle of the congregation, lest ye die: it shall be a statue forever throughout your generations.

Different denominations think differently about drinking wine. There might be some ministers who may drink some wine before ministering. There is a curse of death upon it. And since now we are all kings and priests, this curse applies to any Christian who drinks before going to church.

H) The Curse of Incest

The whole chapter of Leviticus 18 describes in detail

the different kinds of incest that may be committed. At the end of the chapter there is a curse of death:

Leviticus 18:29
For whosoever shall commit any of these abominations, even the souls that commit them shall be cut off from among their people.

I) Curse Upon Those Who Seek Witches and Occult Practitioners

Leviticus 20:6
And the soul that turns after such as have familiar spirits, and after wizards, to go a-whoring after them, I will even set my face against that soul, and will cut him off from among his people.

J) Curse Upon Those Who Curse Father or Mother

Leviticus 20:9
For everyone that curseth his father or his mother shall be surely put to death, he hath cursed his father or his mother; his blood shall be upon him.

The rest of Leviticus 20 contains curses upon adulterers, upon perverted sex, upon those who have sex with animals, upon those who have sex during menstruation, upon those who eat unclean animals, and upon those who have familiar spirits (mediums, witches and channelers).

K) Curse Upon Those Disobedient To the Lord

Leviticus 26:14-17
But if you will not hearken unto me, and will not do all these commandments; and if ye shall despise my statutes, or if

your soul abhor my judgements, so that ye will not do all my commandments, but that ye break my covenant: I also will do this unto you; I will even appoint over you terror, consumption and the burning ague, that shall consume the eyes and cause sorrow of heart: and you shall sow your seed in vain, for your enemies shall eat it. And I will set my face against you, and ye shall be slain before your enemies: they that hate you shall reign over you; and you shall flee when none pursues.

L) Curse Upon a Bastard

Deuteronomy 23:2
A bastard shall not enter into the congregation of the Lord; even to his tenth generation shall he not enter into the congregation of the Lord.

M) Miscellaneous Curses

Deuteronomy 27:14-26	Twelve different curses.
Judges 5:23	Upon those who do not come to the help of the Lord against "the mighty." The mighty are the enemies of the Lord: Satan and his demons.
Jeremiah 17:5-6	Upon those who trust in man and not in God.
Jeremiah 48:10	Upon those who do the work of the Lord deceitfully and upon those who keep back their sword from blood.
Proverb 17:11	Upon the rebellious.

Proverb 20:20	Upon those who curse their parents.
Proverb 30:17	Upon those who mock their parents or hate to obey them.

There are many more curses in the Bible. Sometimes they are worded in such a way that they do not seem to be curses.

2 - Witchcraft Curses

There is a belief in churches that witches cannot put curses on Christians. In my deliverance experience since 1980, I have broken many witchcraft curses that Christians were under. As with any curse, you have to cast the demons out. In the case of witchcraft curses, break the evil soul tie between the witch and the person, and cast out the evil soul of the witch.

Witchcraft curses come to a person through someone whom that person may or may not know, who goes to a witch to put a spell or a curse on the person. Witchcraft curses may also come when a person goes to a witch for any reason, and the witch puts a spell on that person.

And today, witchcraft curses do not even have to come from a witch; they could come from your own son or daughter or a teenage neighbor. Go to the New Age section of a bookstore such as Borders or Barnes and Noble, and take a look at the books offered. You are going to see books that instruct both children and teenagers on how to cast spells. I am sure this instruction is available to them on the Internet also.

Three or four years ago, I had a deliverance "cell" group from the church I attended meeting at my house. Two mothers told me that their high school daughters (different schools) had been asked by schoolmates to become part of a coven at the high school. Another time, an immigrant couple called me to help with their older daughter with whom they were having problems. The daughter told me that her best friend was a witch who belonged to the coven that existed in her high school. This girl came to see me once in Goth garb. This couple finally decided to move back to their native country.

Harry Potter books are now teaching children at an earlier age how to put spells on people. I wonder how many parents are under their children's spells working to get their way on things such as staying up late, or getting more allowance money, or getting their parents to buy them more stuff.

There are different kinds of witchcraft in the U.S. that have come through immigrants. But even before the present immigration explosion, there was Native American witchcraft in the U.S. With the import of African slaves, Voodoo was established in the Louisiana area and Root Work in the Carolinas. Then, there was European immigration that brought other kinds of witchcraft. Later, with the immigration of the Mariel boat lift from Cuba, Santeria was introduced, has grown and is practiced across nationalities, races and social strata in the U.S.

Immigrants from other Latin American countries have brought other kinds of witchcraft. New Age practices have brought an interest in the occult, eastern religions and witchcraft to middle and upper class Anglos.

Because of the freedom of religion in our country, the government has to accept every kind of occultic or witchcraft practice. In Dade County, Florida, Santeria animal sacrifices have been legal for several years.

So, what if you find handfuls of salt strewn in your front yard? Or maybe a banana and black feathers tied with a red ribbon and sprinkled with some copper pennies? What if a woman finds a bra in her lingerie drawer with a cup cut off? Would my Christian brothers and sisters know the significance of these things? Most would throw the item in the garbage can on their way to work and forget about it. The problem is that they might be throwing away and forgetting about the outward manifestation of a curse that needs to be broken.

The first time I confronted a witchcraft curse occurred as follows: I was going to a Hispanic church at the time. One of the ladies of the church had a friend who needed deliverance. She took me to her friend's house. The friend was now a born-again Christian, but in the past she had visited a witch for some problems she had. The friend was compelled to spend almost all her money on gifts for the witch. I perceived that the witch was working this kind of spell on her clients. I did not have much experience then, but with the help of the Holy Spirit, I broke the curse and the woman was set free. Later, the witch tried to retaliate, but I fought back with spiritual warfare, and whatever attacked me left. Later, I found out that the woman who took me there had had the same experience.

I had a problem in my house caused by a witchcraft curse sent by a woman who had joined the church I attended and had come to the cell group I was leading. She claimed to be a born-again Christian who had left witchcraft. Christians, beware!

I ministered deliverance of witchcraft demons that entered a woman when she married a man from Louisiana, who had left a girlfriend to marry the woman. The jilted girlfriend worked a very strong Voodoo spell that came upon not only the woman, but also upon her college-age daughter. One of the demons that came with that curse was living in the armoire in her daughter's room and would disturb her at night, to the point that the daughter was terrified and did not want to sleep alone in her room.

It does not matter what kind of witchcraft it is, we can break the curse in the name of Jesus and cast the demons out. Nevertheless, it would be better to have some knowledge about the types of witchcraft, what they do, what they use, etc.

Pacts With Satan

People who actually get into witchcraft have one or more pacts with Satan. These pacts or contracts have to be renounced and the contract taken away. This is done by faith, because when I demand the pact, I extend my hand, and the demon makes the gesture of putting something in my hand. I don't see anything, but I give it to an angel (which I don't see either) for destruction. It works.

Every time that I minister, I break witchcraft curses. I do not ask the person if they have any, because most people have no idea if they have them or not. In 90% of the cases, they do.

3 - Charismatic Witchcraft Curses

Some ministries call these curses "psychic prayers." Others call them "Christian curses." When I went to Hegewisch Baptist Church to receive deliverance for the first time, I heard about charismatic witchcraft curses, but did not pay much attention to this subject, because I came out of that church with an overload of information. About two years later I became well-informed on what a charismatic witchcraft curse was: someone put one on me!

The Lord Reveals the Curse

Two years before I received deliverance, I attended a weekly prayer meeting that a woman held in Houston. This woman was a member of the Assembly of God church that I attended when I first became a Christian. She almost always had a word of prophecy during the services there. She was a woman of strong character and had her own ministry. I had gone to this meeting for about a year, and then I left because I began to feel uncomfortable there. I left just before I got into deliverance.

When I came back from my first deliverance, I called a lot of friends to tell them what had happened. At the time, I was still a baby Christian and was not aware of the strong opposition to deliverance that existed in some Christian circles. I called that woman, and when she heard my story, she said, "If you had demons cast out of you, you are not a Christian." I answered, "Didn't you see me praising God every week at your meeting?" She replied, "You looked like a Christian, but you are not!"

Two years later I received a call from "M", who was a woman who attended the same church and the same prayer meeting. "M" belonged to the church's choir, and sometimes she sang solos. She had been married to a man who divorced her. "M" told me that she could no longer sing, because she felt as if she had something stuck in her throat; she thought it was a demon.

We met later in the week at a friend's house for ministry. After the preliminary prayers, I spoke to the demon in her throat and commanded it to come out in the name of Jesus. Immediately, "M" had a flashback in her mind (this is common when deliverance is ministered, because it is the Holy Spirit revealing the source of the demon). She remembered one Sunday morning as she was singing a solo at the church, the previously mentioned woman came down the aisle looking for a seat. When the woman raised her eyes and saw "M" singing, she angrily turned around and left the church in a huff. "M" told me that she called some mutual friends to find out why the woman acted that way. The friends told her that the woman had said that "M" had "no right to minister" because she was going through a divorce.

When I heard this, I told "M", "This woman has put a curse on you called 'no right to minister'. " I broke that curse in the name of Jesus, and immediately something very peculiar happened. "M" started having deliverance, but I also started having deliverance! The woman had put the same curse on me. Because the woman believed that Christians could not have demons, she felt that I should not be ministering deliverance to Christians, so she prayed to stop me from ministering.

Charismatic witchcraft happens when Christians pray their own will over someone. This is very wrong. Even the Lord Jesus said to the Father, "*Your* will be done on earth as it is done in heaven." "Not my will, but *yours*."

If you do not know what the Father's will is, do not pray your will, because God will not hear your prayer. Instead, Satan will hear it, and he gets a legal right to send demons to the person you have prayed over. What is the difference between charismatic witchcraft and satanic witchcraft? None! The end result is the same: a curse comes over the person prayed over!

The only exception to praying your will is when your prayer is also the Father's will, such as praying for someone's healing or salvation.

The Lord Reveals Another Curse

Once, a woman called me to come to her house in the evening for deliverance ministry. I told her I did not minister in the evenings (except in a church), and that she needed to come to the place where I ministered. She refused and was very adamant that things be done her way. After the phone call, I noticed I was unusually sleepy during the day, and as I was wondering about it, the Lord told me that the woman had put a curse on me. It was broken, and sure enough, I was delivered from the demon that came with that curse. It appears that she prayed that I would do what she wanted me to do.

Demons Go Back To The Source

The interesting thing about breaking curses is that when the demon comes out, it goes back to the person who sent it. This should be reason enough for us to be aware of how we pray! I know that this might come as an upsetting surprise to most of you, but I will shortly show you the scriptural evidence.

This Kind of Curse is Common

I have broken many charismatic witchcraft curses. It is very common among Christians. Almost everyone I have prayed for has had this kind of curse.

It could happen as innocently as this: a family attends a church. The daughter meets a boy in the church and likes him. They go out once or twice. The mother is pleased with her daughter's boyfriend and hopes it develops into marriage. Then another girl shows up, and the boy also starts to date her. The daughter is disappointed and tells the mother. The mother starts praying that this boy will drop the other girl, or that the girl leaves the church, and that the boy marries her daughter. It sounds innocent, but it is not. The mother is praying her will, and she is sending curses to both the other girl and the boy. This is just an example of a charismatic witchcraft prayer.

It is sad that Christians may even be placing this kind of curse on people they love: mothers praying for their children, siblings praying for each other, etc. Pastors especially need deliverance from this kind of curse.

4 - Spoken Curses

A curse will come to a person when someone speaks evil of that person. The one who places the curse does it either because he has evil in his heart, or because he is ignorant of the spiritual laws of God and talks idly. Idle talk is frowned upon by God.

Matthew 12:13
"I say unto you, that every idle word that men shall speak, they shall give account thereof in the day of judgment."

Idle words are words that we speak without paying much attention to them. We need to think before we speak. The *Strong's Concordance* Greek dictionary defines the word "idle" as, inactive, unemployed, lazy, useless.

When you say something that is unfounded about a person, you are placing a curse. Also, when you prognosticate evil to a person, it becomes a curse. For instance:

"If you keep running like that, you are going to fall and break a leg."

"If you don't study, you are not going to amount to anything."

"Keep eating like that, and you are going to get sick and die."

"That woman is going to make your life miserable."

"If he keeps spending money that way, he is going to end up in the poorhouse."

Parents, grandparents and other relatives need to be very careful of what they say to children. They could be cursing them and not realize it.

I have noticed that some people tend to speak this way. If you have a friend like that, remember to break all the curses she/he says. If your friend is a Christian, explain this spiritual law to him or her. If these friends insist on speaking this way to you even after you have explained the spiritual law, break the curses in their face as they speak them. Perhaps that way, they will be more careful when they speak.

5 - Self-Curses

Self-curses are spoken curses that you put on yourself. You curse yourself when you describe yourself badly, or you prognosticate that something bad will happen to you. People with low self-esteem do this, and their friends should help them realize what they are doing. For instance:

"I look like death warmed-over."

"I'll always be a nobody."

"I'll probably get (insert name of disease here)."

"My relatives died early, so I will probably die early, too."

"I can't walk and chew gum at the same time."

If you do this, confess it to the Lord as a sin and repent. Ask Him to forgive you. Then find a deliverance minister who will break the curses that you have spoken over yourself and get deliverance.

Demons Go Back to the Originator of the Curse

Deliverance ministers send demons back to their source, particularly when breaking any kind of witchcraft curses and casting those demons out. The witchcraft curses are generally death curses. Charismatic witchcraft curses originate through the spirit of control in charismatic witches, and their goal is to control or manipulate the person who receives them. Some Christians, mostly the ones who have not been involved in the deliverance ministry, object strongly to the idea of sending the demons back when breaking curses, citing the Lord Jesus' command to love your enemies and other Scriptures about blessing instead of cursing. These Christians need to understand the difference between our enemies and the **enemies of God**.

Some people may oppose us in work matters, political matters, or family matters. They may not agree with us on any subject, and they may even take steps to stop us from doing something they don't want us to do. They are our enemies, but they are not God's enemies. These are the people we are to love and bless. However, people who are involved in any kind of witchcraft, black or white magic or Satanism are certainly not God's friends. They have made a pact with Satan one way or the other, and unless they repent, **they are God's enemies.**

It may come as a surprise to those Christians who object to demons being sent back to their source to know that they will go back to their source anyway when cast out. They will go back because of spiritual laws that have been written in the Word of God.

The following spiritual law is very much approved by all Christians:

Luke 6:38
Give, and it shall be given unto you, good measure, pressed down, and shaken together, and running over, shall men give unto your bosom. For with the same measure that you mete withal, it shall be measured to you again.

This Scripture is always used when referring to tithes and offerings. However, it refers to more than just money. Jesus had just mentioned:

Luke 6:37
Judge not, and ye shall not be judged,
Condemn not, and ye shall not be condemned,
Forgive, and ye shall be forgiven.

And He continues: "Give, and it shall be given unto you." Thc tcaching was about what you give, provide, or "dish out," and what you receive in return. So, whether it is judging, condemnation or resentment, the "giving" of verse 38 is not necessarily only about money.

Also, it is interesting that the returns are given by men. See the following Scriptures:

Matthew 7:12
Therefore, all things whatsoever you would that men should do to you, do even so to them: for this is the law and the prophets.

In other words, what you give to others comes back to you. What you do to or for others comes back to you. Let's see other Scriptures that confirm this spiritual law:

Proverb 18:21
Death and life are in the power of the tongue, and they that love it shall eat the fruit thereof.

Death: if you love cursing, you shall be cursed.

Life: if you love blessing, you shall be blessed.

Everyone shall eat the fruit of what they say. If you send a spoken curse to someone, the demons that went with the curse will come back to you when they are cast out.

Proverb 17:11
An evil man seeketh only rebellion; therefore a cruel messenger shall be sent against him.

Jeremiah 17:18
Let them be confounded that persecute me, but let not me be confounded; let them be dismayed but let not me be dismayed: bring upon them the day of evil, and destroy them with double destruction.

Psalm 37:14-15
The wicked have drawn out the sword, and have bent the bow, to cast down their poor and needy, and to slay such as be of upright conversation. Their sword shall enter into their own heart, and their bows shall be broken.

Lamentations 3:52, 64
Mine enemies chased me sore like a bird without a cause....Render unto them a recompence, O Lord, according to the work of their hands.

All of ***Psalm 109*** is devoted to teaching us that the evil sent to others will go back to the sender. Read the entire psalm. These are the key verses of the psalm:

Psalm 109:17-18
As he loved cursing, so let it come unto him: as he delighted not in blessing, so let it be far from him. As he clothed himself with cursing as with his garment, so let it come into his bowels like water, and like oil into his bones.

There are numerous Scriptures that show that what a person does to another, be it good or bad, will return to the person. A deliverance minister may command the demons to go back where they came from, but it really is not necessary because it is already a spiritual law.

God Himself could send a demon to a person. The person could be a Christian and not necessarily a person of the world or a pagan. God could send a demon to one of His children, according to their behavior:

1- Saul: Saul was an Israelite, but he was disobedient, and God sent him a demon:

I Samuel 15:10-11
Then came the word of the Lord unto Samuel, saying: It repenteth me that I have set up Saul to be king: for he is turned back from following me, and hath not performed my commandments.

I Samuel 16:14
But the spirit of the Lord departed from Saul, and an evil spirit from the Lord troubled him.

God also sent a lying spirit (a lying demon) to Saul's prophets:

II Chronicles 18:20-21
Then there came out a spirit, and stood before the Lord, and said, I will entice him. And the Lord said unto him, Wherewith? And he said, I will go out, and be a lying spirit in the mouth of all his prophets. And the Lord said, Thou shalt entice him, and thou shalt also prevail: go out and do even so.

2- Job: Job was perfect and upright (Job 1:1). But Job feared trouble (Job 3:25). Satan presented himself before the Lord (Job 1:6), and God gave Satan permission to trouble Job (Job 1:12).

The Enemies of God in the New Testament

Both Peter and Paul the apostles harshly treated those whom they considered the enemies of God. Peter walked with the Lord, saw Him Minister, and heard all His teachings, including the one about loving your enemies. Paul had an encounter with the risen Lord, and numerous visions and teachings from the Lord. They both knew Jesus in a powerful way. The following Scriptures will tell us how they acted:

***1 - Acts 13:6* - Paul**

Barnabas and Paul were on the isle of Paphos, and they went to preach the gospel to the deputy of the isle. There they encountered a Jew, Elymas, who was a false prophet and sorcerer. He opposed Paul in the preaching of the gospel. In the following verses we see how Paul handled Elymas:

Acts 13:10, 11
"O full of subtilty and mischief, thou child of the devil, thou enemy of all righteousness, will thou not cease to pervert the right ways of the Lord? And now, behold, the hand of the

Lord is upon thee, and thou shalt be blind, not seeing the sun for a season."

This certainly was not a blessing; it was a curse of blindness. Paul originated this curse. It was not a curse that someone else originated and Paul broke and sent back!

2 - *Acts 8:14* - Peter

Peter and John, the disciple that was so much loved by Jesus, went to Samaria and laid hands on the believers so that they would receive the Holy Spirit. A sorcerer was there called Simon. He offered them money in exchange for receiving the Holy Spirit and the power that comes with Him. This is how Peter handled it:

Acts 8:20-23
Thy money perish with thee, because thou hast thought that the gift of God may be purchased with money. Thou hast neither part nor lot in this matter: for thy heart is not right with God. Repent therefore of this thy wickedness, and pray God, if perhaps the thought of thine heart may be forgiven thee. For I perceive that thou art in the gall of bitterness and in the bond of iniquity.

Although Simon had been a sorcerer, the Bible says that he believed and was baptized. Even so, Peter cursed him with a curse of death! "Thy money perish with thee" is a curse of death.

Simon, having been in sorcery, understood curses very well. The meaning of Peter's words did not escape him. Simon pleaded with Peter:

Acts 8:24
Then answered Simon, and said, Pray ye to the Lord for me, that none of these things which ye have spoken come upon

me.

Notice that in the two examples above, both Elymas and Simon were sorcerers, although Simon had converted.

3 - *Acts 18:5* - Paul

Paul went to Corinth and stayed with Aquila and his wife Priscilla. When Silas and Timothy came from Macedonia, Paul was pressed by the Holy Spirit to tell the Jews that Jesus was the Messiah, but the Jews did not receive the news and opposed him. This is how Paul handled it:

Acts 18:6
And when they opposed themselves and blasphemed, he shook his raiment, and said unto them, your blood be upon your own heads; I am clean: from henceforth I will go unto the gentiles.

What needs to happen for the blood of one person to be upon his own head? This was a curse of death. In this case, the Jews were opposed to the gospel, but they were not sorcerers.

The Lord spoke to Paul shortly thereafter, and far from rebuking him for cursing those men, the Lord told him:

Acts 18:9-10
Then spake the Lord in the night by a vision, "Be not afraid, but speak, and hold not thy peace: For I am with thee, and no man shall set on thee to hurt thee: for I have much people in this city."

4 - *I Corinthians 5* - Paul

A member of the church in Corinth was a sinner. This

man was having sexual relations with his father's wife. Because the Bible does not call it incest, it is presumed that the father was a widower and he remarried, probably with a much younger woman. The church apparently had not done much to correct this problem. They were wishy-washy. The pastor probably did not even want to talk about it himself and probably did not want anybody else talking about it either. He might have been trying to sweep the dirt under the rug. But obviously, when Paul learned about it, he judged and took measures that the man "might be taken away from among you," as he told the church. Paul was not wishy-washy about it.

I Corinthians 5:4,5
In the name of our Lord Jesus Christ, when you are gathered together, and my spirit, with the power of our Lord Jesus Christ, to deliver such an one unto Satan for the destruction of the flesh, that the spirit may be saved in the day of the Lord Jesus.

Although this was not a curse, it was an extreme measure invoking the physical death of the man so that his soul would be saved. This early death was not only for the purpose of keeping the man's salvation, but also for the purpose of keeping the entire church from sinning.

I Corinthians 5:6
Your glorying is not good. Know ye not that a little leaven leaveneth the whole lump?

The church should not have kept company with the man, but they had continued to do so. At any rate this extreme measure is almost a curse.

5 - Galatians 1:8-9 - **Paul**

In the letter to the Galatians, Paul says that if anyone comes preaching something other than what he had preached to them, let that person be cursed. Paul said it twice. The person who came preaching the "something else" might not have been a sorcerer; he could have been an enemy of the gospel or someone who was confused. It did not matter to Paul; he cursed the person anyway.

6 - I Timothy 1:20 **- Paul**
Of whom is Hymeneaus and Alexander, whom I have delivered unto Satan, that they may learn not to blaspheme.

In this case perhaps he used the same prayer or ceremony that was used in Corinth with the fornicator. It seems that there was hope that the men would learn, so it was not a curse of death.

7 - 2 Timothy 4:14 **- Paul**
Alexander the coppersmith did me much evil, the Lord reward him according to his works.

Paul was quoting ***Lamentations 3:64.***

Guidelines for Ministering Healing When a Witchcraft Curse is Suspected

Recently, a friend called me for prayer because she felt very sick. The Holy Spirit impressed on me that the disease had come through a witchcraft curse. The following is the way that the Holy Spirit guided me to minister, which I wrote down as I ministered. My friend received a lot of deliverance, and she was healed. I am pleased to share this with you, exactly the way I wrote it down:

1- Break the curse in the name of Jesus and command the demon that came with the curse to leave and go back where it came from.

2- Command the following demons to leave: infirmity, sickness, malady, disease.

3- Command the following demons to leave: virus, bacteria, fungus, yeast.

4- Then these: soreness, pain, inflammation, fever, distemper.

5- Now cast these out: "out of focus," stupor, slumber, sleepiness, weakness, death.

6- Cast out these four demons: "anything in the blood that should not be there"; demons attacking the auto-immune system; "foreign invasion of the temple"; uneasiness.

7- Cast out "feel sick" demon; "feel weak" demon; "I don't feel so good" demon.

NOTE: At any time, and frequently, ask the demon, "Who sent you?" The person should know who his/her enemies are.

8- Ask the Lord to send upon the person: energy, strength, well-being and life.

9- Time to praise the Lord!

Blessings

It is so easy to curse someone through the way we pray

or speak! And the curses bring consequences. Just as easily, we can bless people! There are cultures where the children, before they leave the home to go anywhere, ask their parents' blessing. I think this has tremendous spiritual impact. In the same way that a curse negatively impacts the life of a person, a blessing impacts a life positively. Christians need to learn how to bless.

9

Legal Rights of Demons: The Occult

The word "occult" means hidden, concealed, secret, esoteric. It is said that it is called the occult because its practice had to be kept secret and hidden at one time. Obviously, those days are gone, because now we see the occult advertised in all forms of consumer media. The practice of the occult arts has become mainstream with occult practitioners invited to entertain at parties and interviewed by the media to express their opinions about world events.

Because of the openness of these practices today, many people get involved with the occult, and they don't even know that they have dabbled in it. Many tools of the occult are for sale in toy stores and bookstores. Occult books are on the shelves of our libraries for anyone to check out and take home. In Houston there is a nightclub called "Magic Island" in which the entertainment consists of demonstrations of the occult arts.

Many occult practices of generations ago are being practiced today, but with different names. For instance, mediums now are called channelers or spiritualists. Another word for the occult is witchcraft. The word witchcraft could be applied to any activity that could not exist without a link to the spiritual world of darkness.

Any involvement with any aspect of the occult, even when done in ignorance, gives legal rights to demons to enter a person. Occult demons are very strong, and the deliverance from occult demons sometimes are dramatic.

This is an area that needs to be investigated when ministering to someone. The minister cannot simply ask people if they have been involved in the occult. The answer more than likely will be "no". I have discovered that I have to ask about each activity by name, using the list of occult practices in this chapter. The list is not complete; there are practices of the occult that are little known and might not be included on the list.

Some Occult Practices Used as Entertainment

1- "Light as a feather, stiff as a board"

This is a game played by children at summer camps including Christian camps. A child lays down on the ground with a child kneeling on each side of him/her. The kneeling children insert one finger of each hand under the laying child's body. All the children chant, "Light as a feather, stiff as a board." Soon, the two children can lift the child with only their fingers, as the laying child becomes stiff. This is called levitation.

2- The Ouija board

The Ouija board is sold as a toy. Many children get a

Ouija board as a gift, and they invite their friends over to play with it. The board has letters printed in a special pattern. The only other item is a piece of plastic with an arrow at the end. The children put their fingers lightly on the plastic pointer and ask a question. The pointer will move to a letter, then another, until an answer is spelled out.

3- ESP cards

ESP cards were also sold as toys some time ago. Each card had simple pictures, symbols or letters. One child fixedly looks at the card, while the other child tries to get a mental image of what the first child is seeing. This is practicing divination.

4- Tarot cards

Tarot cards are very common. They are sold at regular bookstores and even drugstores. They are used to tell the future or to reveal something that is presently happening of which the person is unaware. It seems that many people who use them do not consider themselves witches.

Years ago, a regular bookstore would not sell any books or tools of the occult. They could only be obtained at occult stores. Now, the bookstores sell all kinds of occult books and tools.

List of Some Occult Practices

- Fortune-telling by Tarot cards, crystal ball, palm reading, tea leaves, clairvoyance, etc.
- Consulting with psychics and mediums, channelers, participating in seances, spiritism or spiritualism
- Horoscopes, horoscope charting and owning Zodiac signs

- Astral projection, soul travel
- Parapsychology
- Hypnosis
- Reading hair, reading eyes (iridiology), reflexology
- Doing drugs
- Tattoos and other cutting or burning of the skin
- ESP, telepathy
- Faith healers and spiritual healing
- Dungeons and Dragons or other role-playing games with occult influence
- Four-leaf clover, rabbit's foot or any "good luck" charm
- Reading books (or listening to recordings) by Jeanne Dixon, Edgar Cayce, Ruth Montgomery, or others involved with the occult, channeling, etc.
- War paint, pow-wows and other rituals from other religions and beliefs
- Walking on fire
- Pyramid power
- Levitation, "Light as a feather, stiff as a board," table-tipping
- Burning incense or candles that have been demonically dedicated or have a special (spiritual) purpose
- Staring fixedly at a candle (until you see something)
- Magic
- Pendulum
- Mind over matter, Silva Mind Control
- Ouija Board
- Automatic handwriting
- Eight ball
- Martial arts
- Yoga, Transcendental Meditation
- Having or wearing the ankh or other occult symbols

- Participating in pagan rituals or ritualistic dancing
- Ekankar
- Water-witching or dowsing
- Witchcraft of any kind: Wicca, Santeria, Voodoo, etc.

This list is not complete. Every day a new occult practice is invented. If someone is bent on obtaining knowledge about the future, about diagnoses, or about a person, the devil is more than happy to help, and the person can use any objects they have available to tell the future. It is not the object used, but the evil spirit behind it that makes it work. In eastern countries the future can be read by the tea leaves left at the bottom of a cup. In Cuba Santeria practitioners read the future by throwing small sea shells on a doily and interpreting the way they fall. If someone wants to read the future using forks and spoons or strings and yo-yos, the devil will happily oblige.

Pendulum

For instance, the pendulum practice uses a string with a weight at the bottom. Holding the end of the string, the person asks a question. If the pendulum moves one way, the answer is "yes"; if it moves the other way, the answer is "no." This practice has been used over the abdomen of expectant mothers to determine if the child is a boy or a girl. Something as simple as a string with a weight attached to the bottom can be used by the devil to answer questions.

Dowsing or Water Witching

Dowsing uses a forked branch. The user holds it with both hands at the top of the "Y" with the other end pointing down to the ground. The person who wants to find the right spot to dig a well walks over the ground until the branch moves in his hands, pointing to the spot . Dowsing has been practiced for many years, and people who use it get upset when told that it is an occult practice. I have found this to be a highly controversial issue, since there are Christians who say there is nothing wrong with it because their fathers or grandfathers used it to find water. Now it is said that what makes it work are the energy lines of the earth or the "chi." The "chi" is an eastern religion concept, used heavily in Feng Shui.

Silva Mind Control

When I had my business, one of my employees had taken Silva Mind Control classes, and she told me that the first part of the training was imagining a room. This was done class after class. The student had to imagine the same room in each class and add something to it, such as windows, floor treatment, wall treatment, furniture, and accessories. When this was completed, the student would "get into the room" and wait for visitors. She said that when she did this part of the teaching, there was a knock at the door, which she opened. There were three men whom she invited in. After that class, the students were endowed with special powers to diagnose diseases. They were told to bring friends who were sick to the next meeting so that the students could diagnose the diseases. The strange visitors were familiar spirits that entered the students when she invited them in.

Automatic Handwriting

The person puts pen to paper and waits until the pen moves on the paper, writing a message. This is similar to the Ouija board, with the person holding the plastic pointer as it moves "automatically."

<u>Ritualistic Dancing</u>

A female medical doctor from Mexico had gone as a child to a dance school which specialized in folkloric dances. While ministering deliverance to her, I discovered that demons had entered her because she had participated in folkloric dancing. The dances were designed for the worship of certain goddesses. Even though she was an innocent little girl, and even though participating in these dances had an educational and cultural motive, and even though her family was spiritually ignorant, the demons were given an open door to enter, and they did.

What the Word of God Says About the Occult

Exodus 22:18
Thou shalt not suffer a witch to live.

Leviticus 19:31
Regard not them that have <u>familiar</u> spirits, neither seek after <u>wizards</u>, to be defiled by them: I am the Lord thy God.

Leviticus 20:6-7
And the soul that turneth after such as have <u>familiar</u> spirits, and after <u>wizards</u>, to go whoring after them, I will even set my face against that soul, and will cut him off from among his people. Sanctify yourselves therefore, and be ye holy, for I am the Lord your God.

Deuteronomy 18:10-13
There shall not be found among you anyone who makes his son or his daughter to pass through he fire, or that use <u>divination</u>, or an <u>observer of times</u>, or an <u>enchanter</u>, or a <u>witch</u>, or a <u>charmer</u>, or a consulter with <u>familiar spirits</u>, or a <u>wizard</u>, or a <u>necromancer</u>. For all that do these things are an abomination unto the Lord: and because of these

abominations the Lord thy God doeth drive them out from before you. Thou shalt be perfect with the Lord thy God.

Isaiah 8:19-22

And when they shall say unto you, seek unto them that have familiar spirits, and unto wizards that peep, and that mutter, should not a people seek unto their God? For the living to the dead? To the law and to the testimony: if they speak not according to this word, it is because there is no light in them. And they shall pass through it, hardly bestead and hungry, they shall fret themselves and curse their king and their God and look upward. And they shall look unto the earth; and behold trouble and darkness, dimness of anguish, and they shall be driven to darkness.

These Scriptures carry biblical curses of trouble, sickness and death upon those who consult with witches or who practice the occult. These curses are inherited by the following generations.

Familiar Spirit: A familiar spirit is a demon that enters a person to communicate to and give the person supernatural knowledge or abilities. There are several explanations about the word "familiar." Some explanations say that the demon is familiar with the person, and some say that the demon is in the family. I do not think these explanations are clear. I believe this type of demon is a principality that has a network of demons that can bring information to him in a flash. Faster than the Internet! This is what a medium or a necromancer has. When someone goes to a medium to talk to a dead person, the familiar gets the identity, personality and knowledge of the deceased from the demons that used to inhabit the deceased. Then, the familiar mimics the dead person. New age channelers also have familiars that function in a similar way. In addition, these familiar demons can give information about historical personalities and relate stories from the past. When a person is put under hypnosis to be regressed, and he or she starts talking as if they were a person from the past claiming to be reincarnated in the present person, it is a familiar demon doing the same thing they do with mediums.

In the Santeria practice, the initiation of a Santero priest or priestess consists of dancing at the sound of Bongo drums (each rhythm invokes a different "santo") upon which the "santo"enters the initiated and becomes the familiar. This is exactly the term they use, "the familiar". In Santeria each initiate to the priesthood could have more than one familiar.

Consulter with familiar spirits: A medium or channeler. A person thought to have power communicating with the spirits of the dead or "ascended masters."

Divination: The art or act of foretelling events or revealing knowledge by supernatural means. Ouija boards, tea leaves, Tarot cards, sea shells, forked sticks, etc., are tools of divination.

Pass through the fire: Walk or pass through flames or walk on hot stones.

Observer of times: Astrologers and horoscope charters.

Enchanter: One who casts spells, one who bewitches. The objective is to "enchant" a person and submit him/her to the enchanter's control. Love potions are enchantments. The word "enchanted" is used to describe someone enamored or delighted with someone or something.

Witches Use Enchantments Over Their Own Clients.

I once was called to minister to a woman who visited a

witch before becoming Christian. The witch that she consulted enchanted her. She explained to me that she had the witch on her mind all the time and was compelled to buy her expensive gifts, spending almost all of her money on the witch. I broke the enchantment and the demon manifested, and it was very much as if the witch herself manifested. It is a long story, but the woman was set free, thanks be to the Lord! It seems that it is a common practice of witches, to enchant their clients to make them come back and give them money and gifts.

Can You Discern Witches Just By Looking at Them?

My husband and I were having dinner at our favorite restaurant. It was mid-week, and it was early, so the restaurant was not very full. I must explain here that I am bilingual, English / Spanish, but to some people I don't look Latin-American. We were seated in a small room, and there was only one other table being used by a man and two young women. All of us went to the salad bar at the same time, and I noticed them. The man was tall and handsome, had on a very expensive suit, and wore a lot of gold jewelry. The women did not seem to be dressed to the level the man was dressed, so I wondered about the mis-match. At the salad bar, they heard me speak in English to my husband, so they assumed I did not know Spanish. Back at the table they felt free to speak very loudly in Spanish. I overheard that the man was a Santero from Miami, and he was leaving for Miami the next day. They talked about the witchcraft work he did. One of the girls called a friend on the cell phone, and speaking even louder, she told the friend that if she wanted a "work" done, she had better hurry up because the Santero was leaving the next day. What a surprise! Anybody would have thought the man was a business man (although perhaps over-doing his jewelry) and not a wizard! I guess all that gold was obtained with enchantments worked over his clients!

Witch: A woman who practices sorcery or is believed to have dealings with the devil. A man is called a warlock or wizard.

Charmer: Close to enchanter. He or she is the one who charms by a ritual or by making charms. A charm is any action or formula thought to have magical power. The chanting of a magic word or verse (mantra), an incantation.

Charms: Anything that is worn for its supposed magical effect, as in warding off evil: an amulet, such as a rabbit's foot, St. Christopher medals, four-leaf clover, etc.

Wizard: A male sorcerer, witch or magician.

Necromancer: One who practices necromancy. Necromancy is the art that conjures up the spirits of the dead and communes with them in order to predict the future or reveal knowledge. Black magic, praying to the dead, lighting candles and asking favors of dead saints belong to this category.

Occult Symbols

There are several Christian web sites on the Internet that show what occult symbols look like. Type "occult symbols" in your search engine and you will find them. Christians need to be able to recognize those symbols, because we should not be ignorant of the wiles of the devil. In Christian homes, I have seen occult symbols in the decorating accessories. I have seen them in the print of the clothing and the jewelry we wear, on the cover of the notebooks children have and in their toys also. You can see occult symbols in graffiti sometimes, particularly if the graffiti is marking the territories of gangs.

Occult Symbols Can Be Deceiving

One day, a young man who moved in the gift of prophecy came to a church I attended. He was wearing an ankh on a chain around his neck. I approached him and asked him to come outside a moment. Then I told him very gently what the symbol represented, what the name of the symbol was, and that it was easily confused with a cross. I suggested that he look it up in the dictionary or Internet. He immediately removed it and put it in his pocket. The next time he came to church, he thanked me profusely.

Most Commonly Seen Occult Symbols

The Hexagram and the Pentagram: These are symbols painted on the floor for the witches' protection when they summon demons. The witches step inside the symbol. These symbols are also used as jewelry, particularly as a pendant around the neck. The pentagram is a five-pointed star inside a circle. When the star has two points up, it is called the Baphomet, and the two points up are the horns of a goat. Sometimes the goat is painted on it, and it is called the goat of Mendes. The hexagram is a six-pointed star, like the Star of David, inside a circle.

The Ankh: The ankh is similar to a Christian cross, but the top is a loop. It is a symbol of an Egyptian god. In jewelry stores, ankhs are displayed with Christian crosses, Stars of David, pentagrams and hexagrams. This is why some Christians get confused and buy an Ankh thinking it is a cross or buy a hexagram thinking it is a Star of David.

The Peace Symbol: The hippie "peace" symbol is really an older symbol, the "broken cross." Upside down crosses and broken crosses are used in witchcraft.

The Anarchy Symbol: The anarchy symbol is an A inside a circle. Anarchy means lawlessness. Rebellious people hate laws; they want to do whatever they please with no restrictions. The spirit of anarchy has always been in the world, but today, I notice more and more anarchy. People do not want to obey the laws of the country, let alone the laws of God. They do not want to obey traffic laws. They ignore immigration laws. Any type of sign posted saying, "Please do not...," has no effect. "No smoking" signs are hated by some smokers who want to do as they please. Anarchy is selfishness to the nth degree.

Blood Sacrifice Symbol: When the legs and the line crossing the A are drawn beyond the circle, and you see it on a wall, door or sign, it means that blood sacrifices are done in that place.

Watchers: The watchers are used in graffiti or by themselves. The watcher is any figure that has eyes. Usually it looks like a skull and bones, but it could have another shape as long as it has eyes. Witches who want to observe a target paint the watcher on a surface (door, wall, fence, garbage bin, etc.) looking directly at the target. Through witchcraft, they put a demon there, and the demon is in charge of observing and telling the witch what they have seen. If you are a Christian walking in the power of the Lord, and you see a watcher watching your house, anoint it, break the power of the witchcraft that put the demon there, command the demon to leave, and then paint over it.

Goths and Vampirism

Perhaps you have seen or know young people who like to dress in black and wear black lipstick and nail polish and very pale or white make-up. They are from the Goth culture. Goths, short for Gothic, originated in a London nightclub in the early '80's. They have their own music and lyrics, and they are fascinated with death. Trying to learn about Goths, I visited a website called "Goths Places to Go." It was full of information on body piercing and tattoo salons, fetishes, alternative bizarre video stores, "World Serpent" cd's, rubber and fetish gear, a metaphysical shoppe, heavy bondage gear, "dark" tee shirts, and cemeteries. It had a list of all the graveyards in their city with driving directions, and photographs of certain cemetery sites and tombstones where Goths like to congregate. The web address is necronom.com ("necro" means death). I clicked on the "members" list and found that all the names were pseudonyms related to death and darkness or names of demons. Some members had their own websites. I clicked on one of them, and it had a picture of Satan as the focal point, and it was all about witchcraft.

The Goth culture was blamed for the Columbine High School massacre, but Goths worldwide have defended their culture saying that they would not do such a thing. The May 1999 issue of *Time Magazine* had an article about Goths, with an inset entitled, "We are Goths and not monsters." One of the Goths interviewed was photographed inside a coffin in his living room. They call themselves "creatures of the night."

Goths are linked with author Anne Rice and vampirism, which seems to be trendy now. The August 3, 2002 issue of the *Houston Chronicle* had news from London about a 17-year old who stabbed an elderly woman, cut out her heart and drank her blood. During the trial, he said he only had a subtle interest in vampirism. The April 24, 2001 issue of the same paper had news about actress Angelina Jolie wearing a glass pendant full of the blood of her then-husband, actor Billy Bob Thornton. She had fresh wounds in her arms, and she explained that she had to cut herself before sex. She would not remove her necklace for the photo shoot.

The Word of God says not to drink blood. Young people coming out of the Goth culture who become Christians will need a lot of deliverance.

Santeria

Santeria, Voodoo, Root Work and Candomble are all related African religions. When African slaves came to the Americas, the British imported them from one part of Africa, the Spaniards from another, the French from another, and the Portuguese from another. This is why there is a difference in the African religions in Georgia and the Carolinas (Root Work), Louisiana and Haiti (Voodoo), Candomble (Brazil), and Santeria (Cuba).

I was born in Cuba, and I remember one day when my black nanny took me for a walk, we came across large trees, the kind that have lianas or thin roots hanging down from the branches to the ground. At the foot of one tree, there was a strange grouping of red fabric strips, bananas and copper pennies. I reached for the pennies, but she pushed me back and was very afraid. She knew that it was a sacrifice to a Santeria Orisha.

Later, when I traveled in the streetcars, passing some neighborhoods I heard the rhythmic sound of African drums, particularly bongo drums. I heard them several times and wondered what they were until someone told me that they were Bembes. Then, I was curious as to what Bembes were.

In my late teens I went to visit a friend. She was a good Catholic girl, educated in the best Catholic school in town. She told me, "Guess where I went last night! Shh! My parents don't know! I went to a Bembe!" I asked her to describe what it was. She told me she and her friends walked into a large room where there was a long table in the middle. All around the table were statues of the santos (Catholic saints). In front of each santo, plates of specific food for each santo were placed. Drums were beating furiously, and people danced around the table. She was told to select a santo and start dancing around the table, and as she came around to the santo, to eat some of the food placed in front of it. She did it and then evidently passed out, not remembering anything else, but her friends told her that "le dio el santo" (the santo entered her). She was laughing excitedly at her adventure. What she did not know (and I did not either) is that a big demon had entered her.

Because of Cuban exiles scattering all over the world, particularly at the time of the Mariel exodus, Santeria has been taken to all of the Americas, the main cities of the U.S. and Europe.

The History of Santeria

Quotes from the Internet documents "What is Santeria?" and "African Religion Syncretism".

- "The Haitian Voodooist, Her-Ra-Ma-E, points out in his book *The Demons of the Voodoo Cult*, that indisputably, the sources of the African religion lie in the Ethiopian-Egyptian Assyrian civilizations where from Voodoo has sunk its roots." This is the root of all the African religions.

- "Santeria or 'La Regla Lucumi' (The Lucumi rule) originated in West Africa in what is now Nigeria and Benin. It is the traditional religion of the Yoruba people there."

- "First of all, Santeria is not a primitive religion. On the contrary, the Yorubas were and are a very civilized people with a rich culture and a deep sense of ethics."

The Yoruba arrived in Cuba with their religion. The Catholic priests there tried to convert them to Catholicism. The Yoruba identified some Catholic saints with their gods, called Orishas (blending gods of one religion with the gods of another religion and considering them the same deity with different names is called syncretism). When the Yoruba worshiped the Catholic saints, in reality they were worshiping the Orisha that the Catholic saint represented. The Catholic priests were satisfied, perhaps because they did not realize what the slaves were doing.

The Yoruba kept their religion intact. In fact, Cuba is the only place where the original African religion was perfectly preserved. In Puerto Rico, the religion was influenced by Indian folklore and French spiritualism. In Brazil, there are four different branches, with Candomble being the most similar to Santeria.

It is interesting to note that the African religions came from Assyria through Egypt and Ethiopia to all of Africa, and Santeria was the least changed.

Bembes are the initiation ceremonies to Santeria priesthood, and it is a honor for an initiate to receive the "santo." When the person is in the trance, the demon will speak through the person's mouth and answer questions from the other priests. My friend did not know it, but she became a Santeria priestess. I have not seen her since, or I would have ministered to her. The strange thing is that to become a Santeria priest, the initiate has to observe several things for a year, one being to dress only in white. However, my friend did not observe any of the rituals, and yet the "santo" entered her.

Santeria is a mystery religion; the secrets are only imparted to the initiate, not the profane. Initiates are sworn to secrecy. The only way to obtain the secrets is by merit. There are several initiations in which the priest going to the next level receives the secrets pertaining to that level, and his knowledge deepens and his abilities grow. The higher level priests are called Babalaos or Babalawos. The sacrifices are candy, fruit, candles, wearing special jewelry, and blood sacrifices, generally of certain animals, but it is believed that human babies are used also.

Mystery religions exist today as they have existed for thousand of years. Masonry, for instance, is a mystery religion.

The list below represents the original names of the Orishas and the names of the Catholic saints that represent them. This list can be used in ministering deliverance to people coming out of Santeria.

- Olorun or Olodumare — Jesus Christ the Lord
- Agayanu — St. Joseph
- Obatala — Our Lady of Mercy
- Oddudua — Saint Claire
- Yemaya or Yemanya — Our Lady of Regla
- Eleggua — Holy Guardian Angel or the Infant of Atocha

•	Orunla	St. Francis of Assisi
•	Babalu Aye	St. Lazarus
•	Chango	Santa Barbara
•	Oke	St. Peter or Michael the Archangel
•	Oshun	La Caridad del Cobre

Do you remember hearing Desi Arnaz singing *Babalu* in *I Love Lucy*?

All the Orishas have "attributes" and a color, and are depicted or portrayed a certain way. They are also identified by bead colors. The Santeros wear necklaces made of small beads in the combination of colors specific to their saint. Some keep the necklace under their clothing. Some business owners, such as restaurateurs that are Santeros, put the beads over the entry door on the inside. It looks like a decorative item, so most people do not know what it means.

The most interesting of the Orishas is Chango/Santa Barbara, because the attributes include a double-edged sword, a castle and thunder. She is depicted with a crown, a sword and a tower by her. The crown looks like the top of a fortress wall. The tower resembles a turret.

The goddess Semiramis is described in the book, *The Two Babylons*, by Bishop Alexander Hyslop, thus: "Semiramis, under the name of Astarte, was worshiped not only as an incarnation of the Spirit of God, but also as the mother of mankind. Astarte is also the name of Rhea or Cybele, the tower- bearing goddess. 'The first,' Ovid said, 'that made towers in cities.' In Syria she was represented standing on a lion crowned with towers. She was queen of Babylon. Ash-toreth, same as Ash-turit, is the woman who made the encompassing wall. The Greek goddess Diana at Ephesus wore a turreted crown on her head, and was identified with Semiramis. She was the goddess of fortifications, and people would go to her when they dreaded an attack on their city."

It is possible that the words turret and tower have a connection to Turit, as in Ash-turit or Ash-Toreth.

Chango is the same demon as previously described. It confirms that the African religion came to Africa from the Middle East and Egypt. This is the same religion that Moses confronted when facing the magicians of Egypt. It is a powerful witchcraft, but the Lord has given us power over all of the power of the enemy, and now we can destroy the works of Santeria in the name of Jesus.

Ministering Deliverance to People Who Have Been Cursed With Witchcraft Curses

One of the first things you have to do when you start the actual casting out of demons is to break the evil soul tie between the person and the witch who cursed him. If someone paid the witch to work the curse, break the evil soul tie with that someone also. Cast out the evil souls separately. Then, each curse needs to be broken in the name of Jesus, and the demons that came with the curse need to be cast out. Different things are used to do works, such as the person's hair, photographs, belongings, even only the name written on a piece of paper. Ask the Lord to send angels to find the item and unearth it, take it out of where it is, melt the piece of ice that it might be in, burn the item or otherwise destroy the works. Cast the demon out that came in with each curse.

Ministering Deliverance to Ex-Witches

Anyone involved in witchcraft has made a pact, contract or agreement with the devil, even if they are not aware of it. For instance, when my friend was told to dance and eat of the offering, she agreed to dance and eat. That was the agreement between herself and the powers of darkness.

When the person that is in witchcraft turns away from it and comes to the Lord Jesus Christ, many times all that has been done is a prayer saying, "I repent of my sins, come into my heart....". This prayer is a general prayer, but for people who have pacts with the devil, there is more to be done. They indeed are saved, because the Holy Spirit comes into their spirits, but their souls are in the grip of Satan. They become unstable because of demonic torment, and their behavior might be strange.

Before ministering, be sure that you pray the prayers of protection at the end of this manual, particularly the ones asking the Lord to send angels to completely surround and cut off any help that might come from the powers of the air. This is very important.

Early in my ministry, I started ministering to a woman who had been a witch and had not told me. I was in a rush and forgot to pray for protection. Satan came from the second heaven and entered her, speaking through her. This is a long story that I am not going to explain here, but I am warning you: don't forget the prayer.

Once you have lead the person into repentance and have prayed the prayers to eliminate legal rights of demons, have the person renounce all pacts, contracts and agreements that were made with Satan or any other principality. Command the demon of the pact to manifest and command him to hand you the pact. Extend your hand to receive it. In prayer, ask the Lord to send an angel to take the pact from your hand and destroy it. There might be more than one pact, contract or agreement, so you need to find out how many were made and repeat the procedure, always casting out all the demons involved. You need to be listening to the instructions of the Holy Spirit. Stop and pray in tongues once in a while.

An Ex-Witch Who Did Not Know She Was Initiated in Santeria

I had ministered several times to a Christian woman who had been in witchcraft before becoming a Christian. She was attending my deliverance school, and we had been studying about Santeria.

During the next deliverance session with her, she happened to mention that when she was a witch, a warlock friend of hers took her to visit a Santero. She said they just visited, and she could not remember much, but she did remember that when she was leaving, they went through the front of the Santero's store where she saw a statue of Chango. She was fascinated with it and had to take it home, so she bought it. Then, when she became a Christian, she tried to get rid of it, but she could not. She could not overcome the desire to have the statue, and she could not bring herself to throw it away. She had to ask a Christian friend of hers to throw it away.

The Holy Spirit told me she had been initiated, and Chango was her familiar. When I asked her, she said no, she had not been through a Bembe, the party to initiate Santeros. In fact, she could not remember much of the visit. I believe she was drugged and dedicated or initiated in some way, because Chango was indeed her familiar. I got Chango to manifest, and we went through all renunciations and pact destructions, and Chango was cast out. Praise God!

Judges 20:9-11
But now this shall be the thing which we will do to Gibeah; we will go up by lot against it; And we will take ten men of an hundred throughout all the tribes of Israel, and an hundred of a thousand, and a thousand out of ten thousand, to fetch victual for the people, that they may do, when they come to Gibeah of Benjamin, according to all the folly that they have wrought in Israel. So all the men of Israel were gathered against the city, knit together as one man.

1 Samuel 18:1
And it came to pass, when he had made an end of speaking unto Saul, that the soul of Jonathan was knit with the soul of David, and Jonathan loved him as his own soul.

1 Chronicles 12:17
And David went out to meet them, and answered and said unto them, If ye be come peaceably unto me to help me, mine

heart shall be knit unto you: but if ye be come to betray me to mine enemies, seeing there is no wrong in mine hands, the God of our fathers look thereon, and rebuke it.

Colossians 2:1-2
For I would that ye knew what great conflict I have for you, and for them at Laodicea, and for as many as have not seen my face in the flesh; That their hearts might be comforted, being knit together in love, and unto all riches of the full assurance of understanding, to the acknowledgement of the mystery of God, and of the Father, and of Christ;

Colossians 2:19
And not holding the Head, from which all the body by joints and bands having nourishment ministered, and knit together, increaseth with the increase of God.

In the Bible a soul tie is described as souls or hearts knit together or attached to each other.

In *I Samuel 18:1* the souls of Jonathan and David were knit together by love. In *I Chronicles 12:17* David said his heart would be knit to them by gratitude.

In *Colossians 2: 1-2* Paul says that the hearts of the Christians in Laodicea were knit together in love. In *Colossians 2:19* Paul says that the members of the body of Christ should be knit together. This knitting together is not physical but of the souls. It is a "knitting together" in love.

All of the above are godly soul ties. The reason for the tie is either love or gratitude in a godly way. However, there are also evil soul ties that are formed when there is an ungodly relationship between two human beings. One of the most common evil soul ties is the one formed by a sexual relationship outside of marriage. A man who frequents prostitutes has evil soul ties with all of them. Evil soul ties are also formed between a witch and the person cursed, and also between the client of the witch and the person cursed.

Evil soul ties are also formed in any relationship that goes bad. Evil soul ties are formed when an employee of a business dislikes a co-worker and tries to make things difficult for that person, for example. They are also formed when a mother does not like the person whom her child marries.

Everyone has both godly and evil soul ties, and sometimes both godly and evil soul ties with the same person. For instance, husbands and wives probably have not only godly soul ties with each other, but also evil soul ties. Parents and children are also a good example of people who have both kinds of soul ties.

Structure of an Evil Soul Tie

An evil soul tie is like a bridge between two people where demons travel back and forth. If someone has a bad relationship with a person and the relationship is over, if the memory of the person persists, or if the face of the person comes to mind frequently, there is an evil soul tie operating. The demons who move in from the other person call themselves "The Evil Soul of John/Jane Doe". These demons <u>cannot</u> be cast out if the evil soul tie is not broken first.

How to Minister

Example: Mary had a bad relationship with Joe Brown. She has forgiven Joe Brown, but the evil soul tie is still there. When you minister, say, "I break the evil soul tie that Mary has with Joe Brown in the name of Jesus Christ, and I command the evil soul of Joe Brown to come out of Mary, in the name of Jesus." If deliverance does not follow and the demons are stubborn, remind them that the evil soul tie is broken, and that they do not have a legal right to stay. You can call the demons henceforth "evil soul of Joe Brown" or just "Joe Brown.."

You should break evil soul ties with parents, grandparents and great grandparents. In cases of witchcraft in the family, you will be surprised to find how strong the soul tie is with the ancestor who was a witch, even if it was a grandparent or great-grandparent whom the person never met.

Note:

- Be sure you call it the ***evil*** soul tie. Don't just call it "soul tie."
- Don't try to cast out the evil soul of (person's name) without breaking the soul tie first.
- Don't break the evil soul tie and forget about casting the evil soul out.

Evil Soul Ties: A Graphic Representation

An evil soul tie is formed.

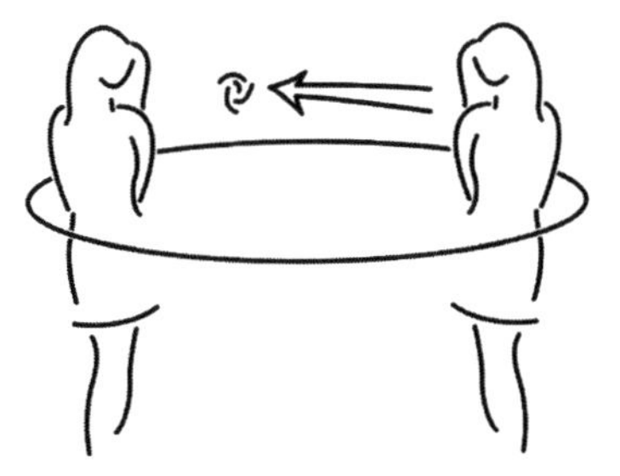

Demons transfer from person x to the other.

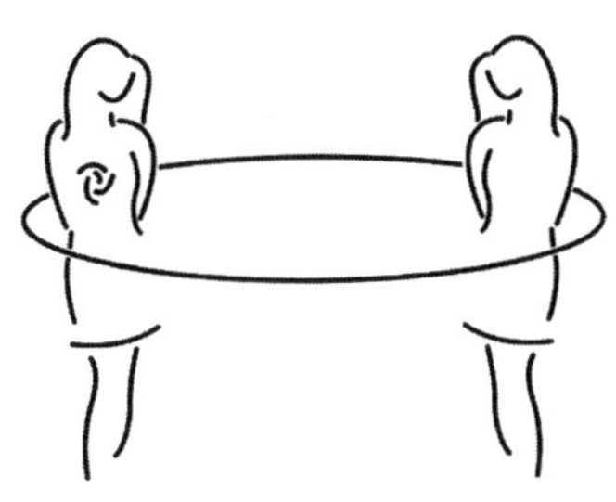

. Demons "nest" in the other person with the name "evil soul of x."

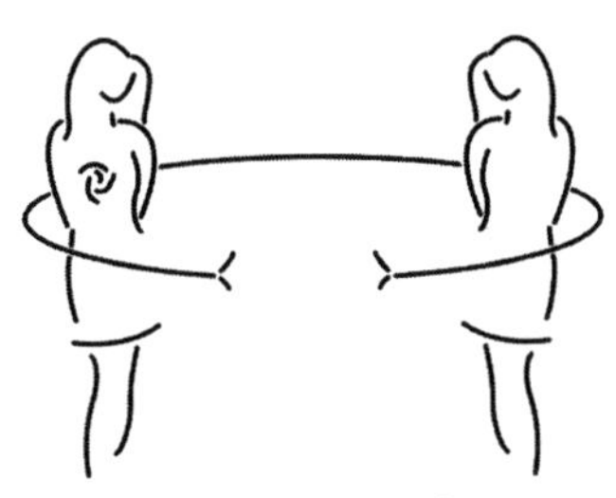

The evil soul tie is broken in the name of Jesus.

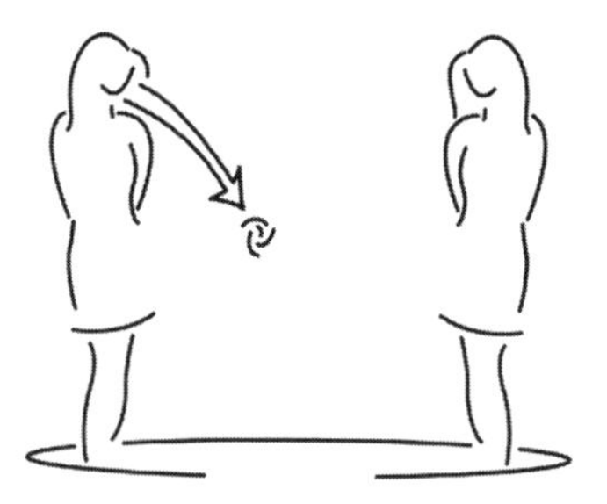

The evil soul of x is cast out in the name of Jesus.

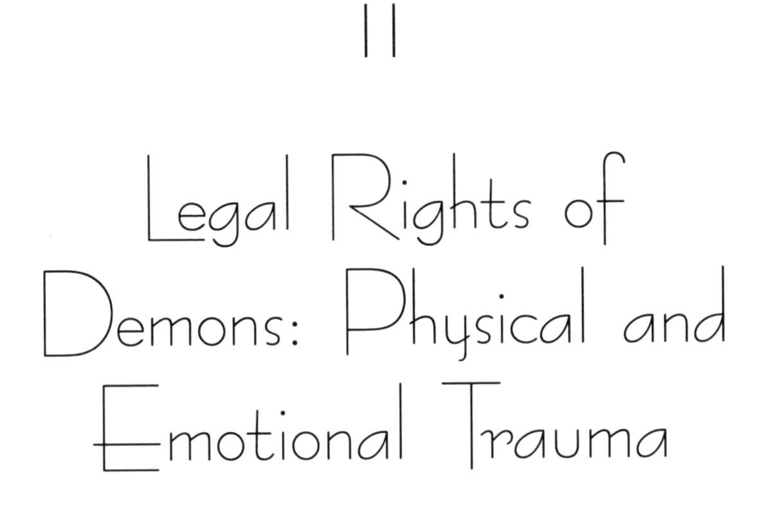

11

Legal Rights of Demons: Physical and Emotional Trauma

Any person who has suffered physical and emotional trauma needs to be delivered of demons called Trauma and Traumatic Shock. Demons such as Fear, Grief, Sadness, Depression, Nervousness and others could have entered during the trauma, but they might be different in each case.

Emotional trauma in childhood together with physical trauma (such as sexual abuse) contribute to the fragmentation of the soul (more about the fragmented soul later). The pieces of the soul keep their attributes of emotions, mind and will, but form separate personalities. Psychologists call them multiples or alters.

Physical trauma, such as being involved in an accident, and even minor traumas, such as cutting or perforating the skin, give legal rights to demons for entering.

Since the Word of God forbids the cutting, perforation or marking of the skin (such as tattoos - even Christian ones!), disobeying these instructions give legal rights to the demons for entering.

Leviticus 19:28
Ye shall not make any cuttings in your flesh for the dead, nor print any marks upon you: I am the Lord.

1- Voluntary cutting of the flesh (piercing).

2- Printing marks on the skin (tattoos).

Notice that one prohibition is cutting, and the other is printing. Christians should not have their skin painted with designs, neither should they wear tribal skin painting. Now, how about tattoos? They are both cutting (perforating) and painting the skin!

Leviticus 21:5
They shall not make baldness upon their head, neither shall they shave off the corner of their beard, nor make any cuttings in their flesh.

1 Kings 18:25-28
And Elijah said unto the prophets of Baal, Choose you one bullock for yourselves, and dress it first; for ye are many; and call on the name of your gods, but put no fire under. And they took the bullock which was given them, and they dressed it, and called on the name of Baal from morning even until noon, saying, O Baal, hear us. But there was no voice, nor any that answered. And they leaped upon the altar which was made. And it came to pass at noon, that Elijah mocked them, and said, Cry aloud: for he is a god; either he is talking, or he is pursuing, or he is in a journey, or peradventure he sleepeth, and must be awaked. And they cried aloud, and cut

themselves after their manner with knives and lancets, till the blood gushed out upon them.

One way that the prophets of Baal worshiped Baal was by cutting their skin. God is not pleased with voluntary cutting or perforation of skin.

Mark 5:5
And always, night and day, he was in the mountains, and in the tombs, crying, and cutting himself with stones.

The above Scripture shows that the demons in the man of Gadara compelled him to cut his skin. Demons love it when you voluntarily cut or perforate your skin!

Exodus 21:6
Then his master shall bring him unto the judges; he shall also bring him to the door, or unto the door post; and his master shall bore his ear through with an aul; and he shall serve him for ever.

In ancient times, a sign of slavery was wearing a pierced earring. Much later, it became fashionable to have one perforation in each ear in which to put discreet little earrings. Now we have multiple perforations in each ear! Whose slave are we?

Cutting and Perforating the Skin Voluntarily or Involuntarily

Because God has expressly forbidden the cutting or perforation of skin, demons have a legal right to enter a person when this procedure is done. This includes:

- Surgery
- Tattoos
- Piercing ears or other parts of the body for jewelry

- Slashing wrists in suicide attempts
- Other cutting or perforating of skin, as for blood-letting, drugs or medications

Once I had surgery on my feet. The incisions made were very small. At the time, I was going to a church where the pastor did not know about deliverance. I asked him to minister to me, and he said, "I don't know how." I replied that I would show him how, and we made an appointment. I had deliverance, but I could tell they were minor demons. Surgery and perforations for blood tests and medications are necessary, and the Lord knows it, but the demons still have legal rights.

How to Minister to Fragmentation of the Soul

In the prayers section of this book, there is a prayer that is specifically for the restoration of the soul in cases of minor fragmentation or fragmentation by witchcraft. In cases of major fragmentation of the soul with multiple personalities in evidence, it is a matter of speaking to each personality and bringing them to the knowledge and acceptance of the Lord as their savior. Then, if they so desire, and the core personality agrees, they are restored to the core personality (see *Psalm 23*). There is much more to this than I can write here, so do not attempt to do this. Instead, find a Christian specialist to minister to these cases. Only experienced specialists can discern between a fragmented personality, a demon impersonating a personality, and a demon.

How to Minister to Perforations and Cuttings

Have the person confess and repent of self-inflicted cuts, and of perforations, cuts and tattoos inflicted by others. Have the person ask God to forgive him. Break the evil soul tie between the person who perforated or cut the skin and the person to whom you are ministering (cast the evil soul out), then anoint with oil the cuts, tattoos or perforations and command the demons who entered through them to come out in the name of Jesus. In the case of surgery or shots, break evil soul ties with doctors, dentists, nurses, etc. and command the evil soul out. Then anoint with oil and command the demons that entered through the cuts to leave in the name of Jesus.

If someone with tattoos has really repented, the person should have the tattoos removed. Wait to minister to him until after the tattoos are removed.

Today, young people are involved in "branding," which is burning the skin like cattle are branded. They are also involved in hanging themselves from hooks threaded through their bodies. These young people are compelled by demons to do the branding and the hanging, allowing more demons to enter. When you minister, you need to inquire about activities such as these in order for them to receive all the deliverance they need.

12

Legal Rights of Demons: Other Religions, Cults and Gangs

1 Peter 1:15-16
But as he which hath called you is holy, so be ye holy in all manner of conversation; Because it is written, Be ye holy; for I am holy.

The call to holiness today is the same as it was yesterday. As much as God loved Israel, the tribes of Israel were banished from their Promised Land because of their involvement with other religions and other gods.

Today, we are surrounded with all kinds of practices of other religions which beckon with promises of mental, emotional and physical well-being. Much of today's alternative medicine is based on practices of eastern religions.

The New Age movement has absorbed and amalgamated eastern religion thinking and philosophy, offering most of the alternative medicine of today.

Exodus 20:4-5

Thou shalt not make unto thee any graven image, or any likeness of any thing that is in heaven above, or that is in the earth beneath, or that is in the water under the earth. Thou shalt not bow down thyself to them, nor serve them: for I the Lord thy God am a jealous God, visiting the iniquity of the fathers upon the children unto the third and fourth generation of them that hate me;

Exodus 34:12-14

Take heed to thyself, lest thou make a covenant with the inhabitants of the land whither thou goest, lest it be for a snare in the midst of thee: But ye shall destroy their altars, break their images, and cut down their groves: For thou shalt worship no other god: for the Lord, whose name is Jealous, is a jealous God:

Joshua 24:19-20

And Joshua said unto the people, Ye cannot serve the Lord: for he is an holy God; he is a jealous God; he will not forgive your transgressions nor your sins. If ye forsake the Lord, and serve strange gods, then he will turn and do you hurt, and consume you, after that he hath done you good.

Romans 11:16-21

For if the firstfruit be holy, the lump is also holy: and if the root be holy, so are the branches. And if some of the branches be broken off, and thou, being a wild olive tree, wert graffed in among them, and with them partakest of the root and fatness of the olive tree; Boast not against the branches. But if thou boast, thou bearest not the root, but the root thee. Thou wilt say then, The branches were broken off, that I might be grafted in. Well; because of unbelief they were broken off, and thou standest by faith. Be not highminded, but fear: For if God spared not the natural branches, take heed lest he also spare not thee.

Christians must stay away not only from the occult, but also from practices of other religions. We must be wary of what we get into; we need to be suspicious and research the roots of any practice before we even touch them. We don't want to be expelled from our Promised Land!

1 Peter 5:8
Be sober, be vigilant; because your adversary the devil, as a roaring lion, walketh about, seeking whom he may devour.

2 Corinthians 6:14-18
Be ye not unequally yoked together with unbelievers: for what fellowship hath righteousness with unrighteousness? and what communion hath light with darkness? And what concord hath Christ with Belial? or what part hath he that believeth with an infidel? And what agreement hath the temple of God with idols? for ye are the temple of the living God; as God hath said, I will dwell in them, and walk in them; and I will be their God, and they shall be my people. Wherefore come out from among them, and be ye separate, saith the Lord, and touch not the unclean thing; and I will receive you. And will be a Father unto you, and ye shall be my sons and daughters, saith the Lord Almighty.

Mystery Religions

A mystery religion is a religion that has followers who are sworn to keep their religion a secret. Secret societies are usually mystery religions (Masonic Lodge, Eastern Star, etc.).

Followers of mystery religions are initiated in ceremonies. If the initiate is considered faithful to the secrecy and other requirements, he will be initiated to the higher levels. So, there are several initiations, and a few obtain the highest levels of the religion. In each initiation, more revelation of the secrets is imparted.

There are mystery religions that do a lot of "good works." The good works attract many to the religion, because of people's desire to participate in the good works. This is why some Christians are involved in mystery religions. Because of the fellowship and the good works, these Christians feel comfortable and don't question the more esoteric aspects of the rituals of the religion or don't consider it a religion at all.

A Christian who comes out of a mystery religion needs much deliverance. Aside from all the general deliverance that everyone needs, these Christians need the following:

- To admit they got involved in an ungodly activity, confess their sin, repent and ask God's forgiveness;

- The breaking of the curses placed upon them for leaving the religion. These are not casual curses, but formal curses written in their laws and spoken over them in a rite;

- To confess, repent and ask forgiveness for each initiation; to reject and break the oaths taken; to have the demons cast out that came with the oaths, done initiation by initiation;

- The breaking of the self-imposed curses of each initiation, and the casting out of the demons that came with those curses.

Christians who know or suspect that a parent or grandparent was involved in a mystery religion will need deliverance ministry as described above. (See Chapter 7, *The Sins of the Fathers*.)

Eastern Religions and the Chi

Many of the eastern religions, New Age and occult practices are based on the Chi. The Chi, also spelled Qi and Ki, is believed to be the "universal energy". This universal energy is thought to run everywhere (including the human body) in linear paths that intersect. The intersections form nodes of energy. The lines of energy and the nodes can be manipulated by eastern religion practitioners.

Some practices based on the Chi are:

- Reflexology
- Acupuncture
- Acupressure
- Martial arts
- Feng Shui
- Tai Chi
- Some massage therapies
- Water-witching or dowsing
- Yoga

Sickness and disease are believed to be the product of obstructions in the lines of energy of the human body, and magnets and other treatments are used to "unclog" the lines.

Hinduism, Chi and Chakras

Hinduism teaches, "Inside every human being there is a network of nerves and sensory organs that interpret the outside physical world. At the same time within us resides a subtle system of channels (nadis) and centers of energy (chakras) which look after our physical, intellectual, emotional and spiritual being. Each of the seven chakras has several spiritual qualities...When the Kundalini is awakened, these qualities start manifesting spontaneously and express themselves in our life." (www.shajayoga.org).

So, when the energy lines intersect, nodes of energy are formed that are called chakras in Hinduism, and the chakras have "spiritual qualities." Does that mean that they are spirits? Why would they have spiritual qualities if they are not spirits?

Yoga

In the practice of yoga, which so many Christians find "harmless" and practice only for the exercise and/or relaxation, there is the danger of the Kundalini arousal. Kundalini is the chakra at the base of the spine. If you have Internet access, type "kundalini" in your search engine and read about it. Kundalini is a coiled serpent, and the Kundalini arousal happens when the serpent uncoils.

The arousal of Kundalini is sought by yoga practitioners, but it can be very dangerous, and there are yoga web sites with advice for people with a "bad" Kundalini arousal. Nevertheless, the yoga instructors call it "the union with the divine" and "god-realization, central to spiritual awakening."

The Kundalini arousal is nothing but a possession by a demon called Kundalini, a serpentine demon. I found a website that described what happened in a yoga class when the Kundalini arose in everybody. It described literal pandemonium. The man who wrote the description was scared to death, and he probably stopped practicing yoga altogether.

Win Worley used to enjoy casting out Kundalini demons. If you have practiced yoga, or other eastern activities such as Tai Chi, martial arts, acupuncture, etc., you will need deliverance of Kundalini and other related demons.

Cults and Gangs

Ministering deliverance to Christians who have come out of cults and gangs is similar to what has been described so far:

- Burn all paraphernalia, books, special dress, etc., first before ministering deliverance.

- If there has been an initiation, have the person acknowledge that he sinned through his participation, confess the sin to God, repent and ask forgiveness.

- Break all evil soul ties to the leaders and other members of the group; cast the evil souls out.

- Denounce any ungodly belief, repent and ask forgiveness, cast out the demons that came with it.

- Break any curses coming from the leaders and other members and cast those demons out.

Part 3

The Practice of Deliverance

But if I with the finger of God cast out devils, no doubt the kingdom of God is come upon you.
Luke 11: 20

13

How to Receive Deliverance

If You Had Deliverance Once, You Are Not Done Yet!

Some Christians hold erroneous concepts about deliverance. One is that it is shameful to have one demon or more cast out. I am still trying to figure that one out. Which is worse, a dirty house or a clean house? The shame is in keeping our demons inside, when the Lord earned for us on the cross, by the shedding of His blood, the deliverance that we sorely need.

I had been born-again for three years, going to church at every opportunity, reading my Bible all the time, and praising and worshiping the Lord every morning for an hour before going to work, when the Lord told me, "You have demons, and you must have them cast out."

Think about that. Every time I came before His throne in prayer, the Lord could see the demons living in me. And obviously, His choice was that I not have them.

The other erroneous concept is thinking that once you have deliverance, you are done. "One sitting, and that is all that is needed."

The truth is that the first deliverance only scratches the surface. My first deliverance was in 1980. At this writing it is 2005, and I still have deliverance. We all continue to need deliverance, since there are things that come upon us such as curses and temptations. The devil will try to infest us with demons throughout our lives.

When I started in the deliverance ministry, I told a Christian friend, who also happened to be a neighbor, that I was now ministering deliverance. She replied with an air of superiority that she had already had deliverance at such and such church. The church she mentioned was a big, important church, and I felt she was name-dropping.

Several months later she asked me to have coffee with her. I did, and she asked me how I was doing with the ministry. I started telling her some anecdotes and situations that I found myself in while confronting demons. She was listening attentively when all of a sudden, she started having deliverance! I spent the rest of the visit ministering to her. So much for "having had deliverance already"!

The first deliverance session cannot get rid of all the demons in a person. Also, there are attitudes that need to change before the person can be delivered from certain demons, and the deliverance minister may need to uncover and explain those to the person under ministry. The first deliverance does open the eyes to the spiritual world, bringing more understanding of the Word of God just because we have had a very spiritual experience, and we taste the reality of spiritual things. This hopefully makes one more conscious of what God requires of us and starts us on a path of desiring to be holier.

It also hopefully humbles us, and perhaps makes us think that, if we had those demons, we may have many more inside of us. In other words, the first deliverance session prepares us to receive more deliverance.

Receiving deliverance is not a right of the Christian. The one who ministers deliverance is a human being; the One who gives the deliverance is the Lord Jesus Christ. Only He knows the heart of the person, and whether the person is sincerely ready to receive. There may be obstacles to receiving deliverance that might be beyond the control of the minister.

Consequently, if a person goes to a minister for deliverance in an attitude of arrogance, unbelief, insubordination or insincerity, such as keeping hidden sins unconfessed, there is not going to be any deliverance no matter what the minister does.

Taking the Promised Land

The reason that we need ministry multiple times is that God delivers little by little. After I entered the deliverance ministry, some Old Testament Scriptures took on another meaning for me. The Scriptures about the war to take the Promised Land spoke to me directly about deliverance.

The land had been promised by God, but Israel had to fight to take it. God was not putting the Promised Land on a silver platter; however, when Israel battled for the land, God was victoriously with them. The Israelites were supposed to cast out all the inhabitants of the Promised Land and not to make any treaty with them or have mercy on them. Then they would live in peace in the land. The capital of the land was aptly named Jerusalem, city of peace.

This was a shadow of things to come: Jesus left His peace with us, but to obtain that peace, we need to fight for it, casting out the demons without making deals with them or having mercy on them.

John 14:27
Peace I leave with you, my peace I give unto you: not as the world giveth, give I unto you. Let not your heart be troubled, neither let it be afraid.

Philippians 4:7
And the peace of God, which passeth all understanding, shall keep your hearts and minds through Christ Jesus.

The peace that the Lord left with us is a peace so deep that the human mind cannot understand it unless it is experienced. Do you have that peace? Do you have peace in times of trouble? If you don't, you have to fight for your Promised Land of peace and cast the inhabitants out of it. Read on:

Exodus 23:23-33
For mine Angel shall go before thee, and bring thee in unto the Amorites, and the Hittites, and the Perizzites, and the Canaanites, and the Hivites, and the Jebusites: and I will cut them off. Thou shalt not bow down to their gods, nor serve them, nor do after their works: but thou shalt utterly overthrow them, and quite break down their images. And ye shall serve the Lord your God, and He shall bless thy bread, and thy water; and I will take sickness away from the midst of thee. There shall nothing cast their young, nor be barren, in thy land: the number of thy days I will fulfil. I will send my fear before thee, and will destroy all the people to whom thou shalt come, and I will make all thine enemies turn their backs unto thee. And I will send hornets before thee, which

shall drive out the Hivite, the Canaanite, and the Hittite, from before thee. I will not drive them out from before thee in one year; lest the land become desolate, and the beast of the field multiply against thee. By little and little I will drive them out from before thee, until thou be increased, and inherit the land. And I will set thy bounds from the Red Sea even unto the sea of the Philistines, and from the desert unto the river: for I will deliver the inhabitants of the land into your hand; and thou shalt drive them out before thee. Thou shalt make no covenant with them, nor with their gods. They shall not dwell in thy land, lest they make thee sin against me: for if thou serve their gods, it will surely be a snare unto thee.

Deuteronomy 7:1-2

When the Lord thy God shall bring thee into the land whither thou goest to possess it, and hath cast out many nations before thee, the Hittites, and the Girgashites, and the Amorites, and the Canaanites, and the Perizzites, and the Hivites, and the Jebusites, seven nations greater and mightier than thou; And when the Lord thy God shall deliver them before thee; thou shalt smite them, and utterly destroy them; thou shalt make no covenant with them, nor shew mercy unto them:

Deuteronomy 7:16-18

And thou shalt consume all the people which the Lord thy God shall deliver thee; thine eye shall have no pity upon them: neither shalt thou serve their gods; for that will be a snare unto thee.

If thou shalt say in thine heart, These nations are more than I; how can I dispossess them? Thou shalt not be afraid of them: but shalt well remember what the Lord thy God did unto Pharaoh, and unto all Egypt;

Deuteronomy 7:21-24

Thou shalt not be affrighted at them: for the Lord thy God is

among you, a mighty God and terrible.
And the Lord thy God will put out those nations before thee by little and little: thou mayest not consume them at once, lest the beasts of the field increase upon thee. But the Lord thy God shall deliver them unto thee, and shall destroy them with a mighty destruction, until they be destroyed.
And he shall deliver their kings into thine hand, and thou shalt destroy their name from under heaven: there shall no man be able to stand before thee, until thou have destroyed them.

Deuteronomy 9:3-5
Understand therefore this day, that the Lord thy God is he which goeth over before thee; as a consuming fire he shall destroy them, and he shall bring them down before thy face: so shalt thou drive them out, and destroy them quickly, as the Lord hath said unto thee. Speak not thou in thine heart, after that the Lord thy God hath cast them out from before thee, saying, For my righteousness the Lord hath brought me in to possess this land: but for the wickedness of these nations the Lord doth drive them out from before thee. Not for thy righteousness, or for the uprightness of thine heart, dost thou go to possess their land: but for the wickedness of these nations the Lord thy God doth drive them out from before thee, and that he may perform the word which the Lord sware unto thy fathers, Abraham, Isaac, and Jacob.

Deuteronomy 20:16-18
But of the cities of these people, which the Lord thy God doth give thee for an inheritance, thou shalt save alive nothing that breatheth: But thou shalt utterly destroy them; namely, the Hittites, and the Amorites, the Canaanites, and the Perizzites, the Hivites, and the Jebusites; as the Lord thy God hath commanded thee: That they teach you not to do after all their abominations, which they have done unto their gods; so should ye sin against the Lord your God.

This is the way the Lord manages our deliverance: little by little. We are to do the fighting, but He is with us and delivers those demons into the hand of the deliverance minister to be cast out.

Preparation To Receive Deliverance

The main thing is prayer. Talk to the Lord, ask Him to reveal the things that you need to get rid of. Fast, at least, the last one or two meals before the ministry. Later on when you have received some deliverance, just fast the last meal before the session.

As you pray, keep a list of the things the Lord tells you or impresses upon you. Write down anything that comes to your mind. Memories that come to your mind are one way that the Lord communicates with you. Write those memories down. Also, write down the reasons why you believe you need deliverance.

If the deliverance minister has given you a questionnaire, answer the questions to the best of your ability, but don't fret if you have difficulty in answering a question. Just inform the minister of the difficulty in answering those particular questions.

On the day that you go to for ministry, wear modest but comfortable clothing. No mini skirts, no shorts. No plunging necklines or tight outfits. Ladies (or men) with long hair should wear it in a pony tail. Ministers need to be able to see the face of the person to whom they minister.

During the Deliverance Session

Don't try to be in control. The minister will ask you to

do (or not do) some things, and you must cooperate with him.

This is what I ask people to do:

1. Do not pray any longer. Do not say the name "Jesus" at all. Most demons come out by the mouth. If you have the name of Jesus in your mouth, the demons will not come out. Surprisingly, some people insist on praying out loud (if you want to pray, pray in your mind). If this happens, I inform them the session has concluded. Just be in an attitude of receiving.

2. Do not command the demons out yourself. If you could have done it yourself, you would not have called the minister. Stay in an attitude of receiving. If anything, agree with what is being done in your mind only.

3. Keep your hands, arms, legs and feet uncrossed. For some reason, the crossing of arms and legs hinders the demon from exiting.

4. Tell the minister what you are feeling or thinking. If something comes to your mind such as, "I hate you," do not be ashamed to tell the minister. Ministers know that it is the demon talking to your mind. If the demon wants to talk, let him talk. Do not try to control the situation or push the demons down, because if you do, you will make things more difficult, and you're working against yourself and your goal of getting the demons out of you.

5. When a demon is being called out, do not say, "I don't have that demon!" If the minister is calling it

> out, it is because the Holy Spirit told him/her to call it out. If you firmly believe you don't have it, you are protecting the demon, and the demon will not come out. As soon as the minister realizes you are not cooperating, the session might end.

A couple of friends ministered to a man I knew. He was hesitant about deliverance, but he wanted it, so I sent him to my friends. They reported to me that although they ministered for a while, there was no deliverance, and when they finished the session, the man stood up and said triumphantly, "I knew I did not have any demons!" Since he had the wrong attitude and did not cooperate, he did not receive any deliverance. Some people go for ministry the same way they go to the doctor for their yearly checkup: to make sure "they don't have anything." With deliverance this attitude backfires, because people do have demons, and when they don't come out, it reinforces their belief that they do not have any demons.

Why is This Demon Here?

When I went for my first deliverance session, demons came out of me for an hour. They came out giving names. The first demon that came out gave his name as "Moroni". I knew who Moroni was: the "angel" that appeared to Joseph Smith, the founder of the Mormon religion. Neither I nor my ancestors had anything to do with Mormonism. Why would I have this demon?

Several years later, I had to go to Provo, Utah on a business trip. I landed in Salt Lake City and was driven to Provo. The client had a certain position of importance in the Mormon church. After the business meeting, I was driven back to the airport by another official of the church. During the trip this official told me all about Mormonism, and what they believed. Now I understood why the Moroni demon had entered me. The demon knew that I was going to have this encounter with this Mormon man in the future, and it had been waiting for the right time to operate, by telling me that what this man was saying was the truth and influencing me to convert. However, it was cast out before "the right time" came around, praise God! Perhaps if I had not had Moroni cast out, I might have become a Mormon.

Ending the Deliverance Session

The deliverance session should not last more than two hours, particularly when there are a lot of manifestations and strong deliverance, because the person being ministered to gets very tired. The minister also gets tired. Both need to rest. If you feel that you need to rest a while or end the session, tell the minister how you feel.

If you do not remember the names of the demons that came out of you, ask the minister to give you a copy of his notes. This list will show your areas of weakness, so you can resist the demons who want to re-enter. Your responsibility is to make the adjustments to your lifestyle, attitudes and thinking that opened the door to those demons. The minister cannot do that for you.

Give thanks to God for what He did for you. Also be prepared to give the minister a good offering. Not everyone is willing to fight demons for you. Be grateful that you found a deliverance minister and that he/she ministered to you. The deliverance minister is an instrument of God, and the offering you are giving to the minister, you are giving to God.

1 Corinthians 9:7-11

Who goeth a warfare any time at his own charges? who planteth a vineyard, and eateth not of the fruit thereof? or who feedeth a flock, and eateth not of the milk of the flock? Say I these things as a man? or saith not the law the same also? For it is written in the law of Moses, Thou shalt not muzzle the mouth of the ox that treadeth out the corn. Doth God take care for oxen? Or saith he it altogether for our sakes? For our sakes, no doubt, this is written: that he that ploweth should plow in hope; and that he that thresheth in hope should be partaker of his hope. If we have sown unto you spiritual things, is it a great thing if we shall reap your carnal things?

Matthew 10:7-11

And as ye go, preach, saying, The kingdom of heaven is at hand. Heal the sick, cleanse the lepers, raise the dead, cast out devils: freely ye have received, freely give. Provide neither gold, nor silver, nor brass in your purses, Nor scrip for your journey, neither two coats, neither shoes, nor yet staves: for the workman is worthy of his meat.

14 How to Minister Deliverance

Who Can Cast Demons Out?

Born-again, Spirit-filled Christians who are not in known sin can cast demons out. If you are in sin, you can cast them out, but the demons will give you trouble, and they will most likely embarrass you by saying out loud what your sin is!

Luke 10:19
Behold, I give unto you power to tread on serpents and scorpions, and over all the power of the enemy: and nothing shall by any means hurt you.

The first time the Lord called me to cast out demons, I was at a church. After the service for the first time in my life, the pastor called me up front to minister. I was confronted by a demon manifestation. I sought help from the pastor, the pastor's wife, and the only elder, in that order.

They did not seem to see me waving at them, as if I were invisible. The Lord told me, *"I am with you, and I am enough!"*

If you are a born-again, Spirit-filled Christian, the Lord has already given you power to cast out demons. Besides, He is with you, and He is enough!

You need to know who you are in Christ. If the demons realize that you know your authority in Jesus, they will not give you much trouble when you minister deliverance.

New at Deliverance

The demons know when you are new at ministering deliverance, so they try to intimidate you. When I was new, a demon looked at me squarely in the face and asked me, "Who are you?" The demon had an attitude as if he were saying, "Who are you to cast me out?" But since the question was, "who are you," I thought, "I am supposed to be asking their names, not vice-versa!" The Holy Spirit promptly brought to my mind what to say. I replied, "I am a child of God!" Bingo! The arrogance in the demon's attitude quickly vanished.

As you continue gaining experience, they stop the intimidation. And as you continue ministering, the demons get to know you. I mentioned before that I believe demons have a communications network that is faster and better than the Internet. Now, I find demons who know who I am. In fact, I have been training my daughter in the ministry, and when the time for hands-on practice came, a demon she was casting out told her, "Stop acting like your mother!" He knew I was her mother. There are a lot of things demons know about us humans.

At Hegewisch Baptist Church, the late Pastor Win Worley used to cast out demons "right and left." He trained many people in the ministry. His whole congregation knew how to minister deliverance. During workshops, when visitors would come for deliverance and education, the congregation would minister to the visitors, and when a demon refused to leave, all that was needed was to say, "I will ask Pastor Worley to come and help." The demon would reply, "No! Not Worley! Not Worley!" The demons knew him.

Let's Start Ministering

This is the structure of a deliverance ministry session:

- Talk to the person to obtain information about their spiritual background, childhood traumas, involvement with the occult, and reasons why they are seeking deliverance at this time. If a questionnaire has been sent and received, go over the questionnaire and clarify answers. Have a notebook designated for the ministry, and take notes.

- Find out how much the person knows about deliverance. If necessary, explain what will be happening, and what they should expect.

- Come to the Lord in prayer, then pray the prayer to ask for protection and the prayers to take away legal rights (see the chapter on prayers).

- Explain to the person that now they should not pray any longer. Tell the person not to cross hands, arms, legs or feet, and to report to you any feelings in his/

her body or any thoughts that come to his/her mind. Make it clear that he/she needs to cooperate with you completely.

- Face the demons in the person, and command them to be ready to come out. Start by breaking evil soul ties and casting those demons out. Continue by breaking curses and casting those demons out. If the Holy Spirit shows you otherwise, do what He wants. Keep taking notes.

- After some time of deliverance (not more than two to three hours), bind the remaining demons in the name of Jesus. Ask the Lord to send angels to bind and gag those demons, put them in cages and read them Scriptures day and night until the next deliverance session. When you pray this, some demons might come out because they do not want to be put in cages.

When talking to the person, try to uncover as much pertinent information as you can. Go down the list of occult practices and ask, one by one, if he has had anything to do with it. Some people are not aware of the danger of the occult, so they take it lightly. You may have to define what each of the items on the list is. When they realize what you are talking about, they might even tell you things they did that are not on the list!

Be prepared for people who are used to visiting psychologists. They are used to relaxing and talking and not listening. They will try to follow the same pattern during the deliverance session. Be careful, as this also may be a demon trying to block, derail or delay the deliverance session. You will have to ask pertinent questions and cut off the conversation when you feel you have enough information to start ministering.

After saying the prayers, explain to the person how to cooperate. I have discovered some people cannot obey these instructions. Repeat them to make sure they understand clearly. If they still do not cooperate, there are demons of rebellion and unsubmissiveness in them. Sometimes the best thing to do is to stop ministering and tell them to come back when they feel they can cooperate.

Flashbacks

Sometimes the Lord will bring a memory or flashback to the person's mind. It could be a face, a name, or something that happened to them. What the Lord brings to mind is important, because it is always directly related to the demon you are trying to cast out. Be sensitive to these visions or memories, and do not dismiss them.

One of my students was trying to cast out a demon of a particular disease from a woman. The demon was resisting being cast out. Suddenly, the woman started crying her eyes out. The Lord had brought the face of her grandmother before her. That was all. She got shook up, because her grandmother had been dead for some time. She did not understand why she was seeing her, and she was upset. The student called me to help with the situation. I asked the woman why she was crying, and when she told me, I discerned that the woman had inherited the disease from the grandmother. We broke the evil soul tie, and we led the woman in praying and asking forgiveness for the sins of the fathers. After she understood that it was God who was giving her the vision, she calmed down.

Men to Men, Women to Women

Men should minister to men, and women should minister to women. The reason for this is that women feel more comfortable being ministered to by a woman, and men feel more comfortable being ministered to by a man. There are private things a woman shouldn't tell a man, and vice-versa. Another reason is that a spirit of lust might manifest. Laying on of hands during the deliverance ministry should be woman to woman and man to man.

An exception is a pastor, because of his spiritual authority over his congregation. However, when a male pastor ministers to a woman, there should be another woman present all the time. Another exception is fathers ministering to daughters, mothers ministering to sons. Parents have spiritual authority over the demons in the children.

Demons Take Advantage

I teach women never to go to see a pastor without the accompaniment of a woman friend. One woman I taught did not take my advice, and she went by herself to a pastor for deliverance. She angrily called me later to tell me that the man had made advances to her.

I repeat: never go see a pastor or minister without a friend. The pastor needs to have someone with him also, preferably his wife. In deliverance sessions demons arise and take advantage of the situation, particularly lust demons. Take precautions.

Pastors, there are women who have been very hurt by men and have gone through painful circumstances which have fragmented their souls. The fragmentation produces other personalities and a wicked flip-side personality. The wounded woman comes to your church and behaves as an angel, because she is in her core personality, but the flip-side wants to hurt men. If this woman comes to you for ministry, and you are alone with her, the flip-side personality will try to seduce you. Take my advice: never minister to women alone; have your wife with you, or a trusted female friend, if you are single.

If this incident happens to you, remember that this woman needs a lot of compassion, restoration of her soul and much deliverance. If you get angry, get angry at Satan, not at the woman.

Not by Yourself

Never minister to another by yourself, unless the person has received a lot of deliverance already, or you know the person and are sure that there will be no violent manifestations. Two or three people ministering is better, and it's a good idea to have a witness anyway. Some manifestations might be violent, and help will be needed to restrain the person. Remember, Jesus sent the disciples out in pairs.

Love and Compassion

When restraining someone, be sure the person does not get hurt. Some deliverance ministers seem to "manifest" themselves, becoming violent and abusive with the people they minister to. It seems to be a lack of love. The minister should have compassion for the person under ministry.

Once, I was in a church to which I was trying to bring a knowledge of deliverance. The pastor asked a friend who also had a deliverance ministry to "check me out." We met at the church, and I passed the test. In the evening the woman had the pulpit. She spoke about deliverance and then ministered. I was keenly observing to see if I could learn something new. What I did see was this: while the woman was ministering to a young girl, a demon manifested who did not want to look at the minister. The woman wanted the girl to look at her, so she took the girl by the hair and yanked her head up violently. I thought for sure the minister had scalped the girl!

Some years ago, I read that someone was killed by the way they were ministered deliverance. People who want to be deliverance ministers should have all their major demons cast out first. If you do not have patience, perseverance, love and compassion, do not minister deliverance.

Are Manifestations Necessary?

I have heard and read a lot of controversy about the need for manifestations. I believe it is not a matter of need; manifestations just happen!

Some ministers tell me they cast out demons without manifestations. This occurs because the really big ones did not manifest and were not cast out. The only demons that leave without manifestations are the smaller ones in the hierarchy.

If you read the chapter on *The Deliverance Ministry of Our Lord*, you must have seen that demons manifested when Jesus was around, and He never suppressed their manifestations.

John 13:16
Verily, verily, I say unto you, The servant is not greater than his lord; neither he that is sent greater than he that sent him.

John 15:20
Remember the word that I said unto you, The servant is not

greater than his lord. If they have persecuted me, they will also persecute you; if they have kept my saying, they will keep yours also.

An Urgent Call

One day a person, who had been trained in deliverance by a person whom I had trained, saw me in a church that I was visiting. He told me with an air of pride that the Lord had told him that He was anointing him with such a powerful anointing to cast out demons that he "would not need the demons to manifest," and they would come out right away.

I know the Lord can do anything He wants to do with anybody at any time that He wants to do it. However, I was a little surprised, but I said "Praise the Lord," and congratulated the person. The only reservation I had was his air of pride.

A few months later my husband and I moved to another house. The move was complicated, and I did not connect the telephone answering machine for a few days. When I finally connected it, I found an emergency call that I had not realized was on the tape from this "anointed" person. He was casting out a demon, ran into problems, and wanted me to come over right away to help him. Too late. I wondered what happened to the special anointing!

How to Discern a Manifestation

When you start commanding the demon out, observe the eyes and the expression on the face of the person. Keep hair clips handy to pull the hair away from the face. Hateful looks, expression changes, shaking, etc., means the demon has surfaced.

The bigger demons may talk to you, or throw the person to the floor. At this point, command the demon out in the name of Jesus. If they do not come out, repeat, "The Lord Jesus Christ rebuke you." Use this as a ramrod. You have to barrage the demons with Scriptures reminding them of what Jesus did on the cross, and that Satan is defeated. Tell them to look around and see the angels who are waiting for them to come out. Ask the Lord to send angels with chains to bind the demon and pull the ends of the chain tight. Tighter! Tighter! Ask the Lord for the angels to bring the black flames of Tartarus for the demons to see, etc. Don't stop talking. You can switch to praying in tongues and listen to what the Holy Spirit will tell you.

Most demons do not like to look into your eyes. They may shut the person's eyes in an effort to avoid looking at you. Ask the person to keep looking at you, or just command the demon to look at you. This will weaken them.

Grill the demon with questions: What is your name? How did you enter? What is your function/ work/job in there? Who is your boss? How long have you been there? What are your plans? Let the demon talk, and listen. He may be giving you the clues to cast him out! He might indicate how he entered. He might be saying what his work is.

Never stop talking, quoting Scripture, commanding him to come out, questioning him, and saying, "The Lord Jesus Christ rebuke you!" Drive the demon crazy!

Jude 1:9
Yet Michael the archangel, when contending with the devil he disputed about the body of Moses, durst not bring against him a railing accusation, but said, <u>The Lord rebuke thee.</u>

Do Not Insult the Demons

As you see from the previous Scripture, we are not to insult the demons. Do not call them names. Jesus did not insult them or call them names.

2 Peter 2:10-12
But chiefly them that walk after the flesh in the lust of uncleanness, and despise government. Presumptuous are they, selfwilled, they are not afraid to speak evil of dignities. Whereas angels, which are greater in power and might, bring not railing accusation against them before the Lord. But these, as natural brute beasts, made to be taken and destroyed, speak evil of the things that they understand not; and shall utterly perish in their own corruption;

Do Not Scream at The Demons!

I almost feel like screaming this one out! Demons have very good hearing. They can hear a whisper. You can tell how much experience a minister has by the loudness of his/her voice. The less experience, the more he/she screams. You can speak in a very low voice and demons will have to obey. Remember who is the One who gives deliverance: It is not us, or our loud voices!

Isaiah 30:15
For thus saith the Lord God, the Holy One of Israel; In returning and rest shall ye be saved; in quietness and in confidence shall be your strength.

I have seen deliverance ministers screaming in the person's ear. This is abusive, and if they damage the person's ear, they may be liable for the damage.

The Princes

The bigger, higher-ranking demons try not to manifest, because they know that if they manifest, they will be easier to cast out. When they manifest, they will look at you and say:

- They will destroy you.
- They will never be cast out.
- You will get tired before they do.

Do not be afraid; remember that the Lord is with you. I have cast out many of these kinds of demons. It may take a little bit longer with a little more work, but they will lose the battle.

Ephesians 6:12
For we wrestle not against flesh and blood, but against principalities, against powers, against the rulers of the darkness of this world, against spiritual wickedness in high places.

Use the Scriptures

The word of the Lord is a sharp sword that separates soul from spirit.

Hebrews 4:12
For the Word of God is quick, and powerful, and sharper than any twoedged sword, piercing even to the dividing asunder of soul and spirit, and of the joints and marrow, and is a discerner of the thoughts and intents of the heart.

Ephesians 6:17
And take the helmet of salvation, and the sword of the Spirit, which is the Word of God:

Revelation 1:16
And he had in his right hand seven stars: and out of his mouth went a sharp twoedged sword: and his countenance was as the sun shineth in his strength.

I found some Scriptures that demons particularly hate. They are in Chapter 17. You could learn them by heart, or you can copy and laminate that page to have them handy when you minister.

Take a Prayer Break

Depending on the situation, it will be necessary to stop and analyze why the demon does not come out. Why is the demon there? What made it come in? Does it have to do with another person? (Break soul ties.) If the demon has said he has been there for a long time, it means it is a hereditary demon.

Ask the person to pray. It may be that acknowledgment, confession, and repentance of a sin is needed, asking God for forgiveness. It may be that a curse needs to be broken. It may be that the person needs to repent for the sins of the fathers.

It may be that a revelation from the Holy Spirit is needed. Pray in tongues.

The Anointing Oil

Please do **not** use the anointing oil sold at Bible stores. Some ministries also sell anointing oil. If the oil has been mixed following the formula in the Bible, it carries a curse with it. Here is the Scripture again that is in chapter 8, section C, of this book:

Exodus 30:29-33

And thou shalt speak unto the children of Israel, saying, This shall be an holy anointing oil unto me throughout your generations. Upon man's flesh shall it not be poured, neither shall ye make any other like it, after the composition of it: it is holy, and it shall be holy unto you. Whosoever compoundeth any like it, or whosoever putteth any of it upon a stranger, shall even be cut off from his people.

Use only plain, fresh olive oil. I put mine in a small plastic bottle that can dispense a drop at a time when I squeeze it.

Pray for the oil in front of the manifesting demon so they know what you are praying for. Ask the Lord to put His Holy Spirit in the oil and make it an anointing oil powerful to cast out demons. (When you use the oil for another person, pray again.) Then, anoint the forehead or wherever the Holy Spirit indicates.

I like to anoint under the nose of the person, so it gets inhaled. The demons hate it, so I may put the bottle under the nose.

The Third Eye

When the person has been involved in the occult, that person has developed the "third eye". The third eye is located between the eyebrows and just a little above them (about the same spot where the Hindus paint the little red dot). Anoint the spot with oil, command the third eye to be blinded, then ask the Lord to command the angels to pry it open and pull out all the demons that entered through it. Command these demons to come out.

The Burning Oil

Once, a friend wanted me to minister to a friend of hers. Her friend was a difficult and demanding person. As I ministered, I put the bottle of oil under her nose. She started to protest, make faces and say that the oil was revolting and nauseating her because it was rancid (it was not). I asked my friend if she had olive oil in the house. She did not. I asked for any other cooking oil. She ran all over the house and finally brought a bottle of mineral oil. I prayed over the mineral oil just as I had prayed over the olive oil. The Lord heard that prayer, because when I put it under the woman's nose, she screamed saying that the oil was burning her.

This woman was not ready for deliverance. She could not tell where she finished and her demons began. She attributed the reaction of the demons to herself. In other words, she and the demons were one. I hope she has learned to discern and differentiate her own soul from the demons.

Head Coverings for Women

Demons hate for women to cover their heads, particularly the Jezebel demon. If you cover the person's head, Jezebel will immediately grab the scarf and throw it to the floor. At Hegewisch Baptist Church, all the ministering women cover their heads when they cast out demons. It is a good practice.

Demon or Personality?

Sometimes a personality will surface rather than a manifesting demon, if the person has had traumas that have fragmented his/her soul. You need to recognize a personality. Personalities, of course, are not cast out but, if you do not recognize them, you may be trying to do so. Unless you have been trained to minister to multiple personality cases, do not attempt to do so.

Sometimes the person is so in tune with his/her demons that they cannot discern the difference between themselves and a demon, and they believe that what is going on with them is their own personality. Demons like to deceive the person into believing that they are his/her personality.

"I'm Not a Demon"

I ministered to a young woman one day who had plenty of deliverance. A few days later, she called to tell me that the demon that she really wanted cast out had not come out. She told me that she was very shy, and she wanted to get rid of the shyness demon.

We met again, and I started speaking to this particular demon, commanding him to manifest and come out. Nothing was happening. No manifestations. The woman was cool as a cucumber looking at me. So strange... not like the first time we met! I stopped trying, and she took the opportunity to explain: "I am so shy that I blah, blah...I was so shy when I was little that I blah, blah...then when I was in high school I was so shy that I blah, blah...I have been shy all my life...I am so shy that I blah, blah..." I was listening to this and getting uncomfortable. Then, the Lord spoke to me and said, *"Tell her that she is not shy, that I did not make her shy, that it is a demon that has convinced her that he is her personality!"*

I immediately told her verbatim what the Lord told me. I could see in her eyes that she understood (the Word of God separates soul from spirit) and Bingo! The demon manifested right away and told me, "I am not a demon! I am her personality!" It took a little while, but because she did not believe the demon any longer, she was set free of that demon. Praise God!

Strongholds: ***You shall know the truth and the truth shall set you free!***

The young lady of the story above had a stronghold: the belief in a lie. It could have been a demon that told her the lie, or it could have been a person who told her the lie (it could even have been a pastor or evangelist). The person who told the lie was also deceived by a demon. This woman chose to believe the word of the Lord, so the stronghold was pulled down.

To minister to a person with a stronghold, you cannot start by casting the demon out. First, you must get the truth to penetrate the stronghold in order to destroy it. Then, you can cast out the demon. It is up to the person to choose what to believe. There is nothing much you can do, if the person prefers to believe the lie.

A student of a Bible school came to me for deliverance. The session was going fine with several demons cast out, until a demon called Stubborn manifested. This one was not coming out. The flow of deliverance stopped. I tried to make her confess stubbornness as a sin, repent, etc., but she started talking about her family. "My family is very stubborn," she said, with a growing air of pride. "Uncle Harry was very stubborn. My Grandad was also very stubborn." As she kept talking about the family, I could tell the family considered stubbornness a great quality. By now, she had her nose up in the air. This was the end of that deliverance session, because she lost her interest in being set free. She had a stronghold because she believed the family lie that stubbornness was a great personality trait or quality to have. She confused stubbornness with the better quality of perseverance or tenacity.

2 Corinthians 10:3-5

For though we walk in the flesh, we do not war after the flesh: (For the weapons of our warfare are not carnal, but mighty through God to the pulling down of strong holds;) Casting down imaginations, and every high thing that exalteth itself against the knowledge of God, and bringing into captivity every thought to the obedience of Christ.

Be Prepared: Demons Do Not Come Out Gracefully

What do you expect from a demon? I believe that this is the reason most churches do not want anything to do with deliverance: it's just not "politically correct" behavior.

Demons come out in different ways. Minor demons come out in tears, through runny noses or through big yawns. In my first deliverance session, I spent the whole time screaming.

Occult demons come out of the mouth, vomiting a clear mucous substance commonly called "the demon's nest." Sometimes the substance is not clear, and not odorless. Seldom is anything that the person has eaten vomited. A few people have to run to the bathroom. In my experience, vomiting or having to run to the bathroom occurs when the person has received many witchcraft curses.

I have gone to meetings where I have heard many anointed preachers and evangelists deriding this aspect of deliverance, making fun of the buckets given at the door of certain deliverance meetings. These are people who are ignorant of, or who have glossed over parts of the Gospel and have never ministered deliverance. How sad for them. Not only have they not completely obeyed the Lord, but they also will have to give an account of every idle word they have spoken.

Matthew 12:36-37
But I say unto you, That every idle word that men shall speak, they shall give account thereof in the day of judgment. For by thy words thou shalt be justified, and by thy words thou shalt be condemned.

A Jezebel demon told us about the angels surrounding us during a session. I could see her grimaced facial expression when I asked the Lord to send the angels to bind her with chains and tighten them. The angels were there, and they were helping with the ministry. The angels do not make fun of the buckets.

Why Is It That Sometimes There Is No Deliverance?

If there is no deliverance when you minister, do not feel that you are not "anointed". You are only an instrument of the Lord. He is the One who gives deliverance. If there was no deliverance, it is because He did not give it.

The Devil would like you to think that you cannot cast out demons, that you are not anointed, that you are not good enough, that you are getting into something too big for you, etc. The Devil is in the business of fighting deliverance and trying to stop Christians from casting out demons.

I can minister to one person who has lots of deliverance with manifestations, demons talking to me, etc. Then someone else comes along. I am sitting in the same chair, wearing the same dress, and saying the same things, and there is no deliverance. What makes the difference? Not me!

You have already read about these two hindrances to deliverance:

- The person being ministered to believes that he/she does not have any demons, and just came "to be sure"; and

- The person has believed a lie, which is a stronghold that needs to be destroyed first.

Other hindrances could be that the person:

- Is not being sincere about their sins; he/she is living in sin but does not tell you;

- Is not ready for deliverance; the Lord knows this, so He does not let it happen;

- Is too nervous;

- Wants to be in control and thus cannot receive;

- Has accursed objects in his/her home.

Accursed Objects

Ideally, the person who comes for deliverance should have already disposed of all accursed objects. But this is not the case the majority of times, mainly because people do not recognize what an accursed object is, and sometimes when we tell them, they do not believe it.

These objects include statues or images of idols or "saints." Books on the occult. Objects used in the practice of the occult. Anything with symbols of the occult, such as clothing, posters, or decorative accessories. Items used in the rituals of other religions rituals. Sometimes they are things that no one would consider particularly evil.

The Big Doll That Didn't Sleep

Many years ago, a lady from the church I attended wanted me to visit her. She asked me to walk through her house and see if there was anything she needed to get rid of. I walked through the house, and nothing really bothered me until I entered her teenage daughter's room. In a corner there was a big doll propped against the wall. I felt evil emanating from that doll. I felt silly, but I said, "That doll!" The daughter said, "Mom! That doll falls down every night and wakes me up! I am getting tired of it!" The doll did not do that during the daytime. They burned the doll.

Showrooms

I used to be a commercial space planner and interior designer, visiting designer showrooms, and I can say that there are many accursed objects in those showrooms. But you don't have to go to a designer showroom to find or be able to buy these objects.

Designers and their clients seem to be fascinated by idols and by items used in rituals. Not only are some decorative accessories accursed, but many antiques also come loaded with demons. Some items can be anointed and the demons cast out, but other items, because of what they represent, or the carvings they have, or because of the use they had, cannot be exorcized.

These items must be burnt. If they cannot be burnt, they should be destroyed otherwise. Do not attempt to sell those items, nor give them away as gifts.

When I went for my first deliverance, I discovered that I had accursed objects in my house. The Lord showed the lady who was ministering to me those objects. In fact, before that, the Holy Spirit had been trying to show me at home, but I wasn't paying attention.

I wrote a book about my deliverance from the demons that those objects brought to me, and how one of them resisted being burned. One of the demons that entered me was a werewolf demon. The book I wrote was edited and published by Win Worley. For more information, obtain booklet #39, *Idols And Images, The Second Commandment,* from WRW Publications.

"I Don't Have Any Place to Go!"

Some demons do not want to leave saying that they do not have a place to go. They are lying, and they want you to have pity on them and leave them where they are. I just tell them that the angels will take them where they need to go.

Where Do Demons Go?

Some people fear being around when someone is having deliverance because they think the demons cast out will enter them. They fear being around when someone is having deliverance. Other people are afraid to receive deliverance because they believe seven more demons will enter according to Scripture. As we have seen, demons do not enter a person unless they have legal rights to do so. The person who has given legal rights is prepared or ready to receive demons.

The following Scripture is the one inspiring the fear of demons entering. Many people have quoted it to explain why they do not want deliverance.

Matthew 12:43-45
When the unclean spirit is gone out of a man, he walketh through dry places, seeking rest, and findeth none. Then he saith, I will return into my house from whence I came out; and when he is come, he findeth it empty, swept, and garnished. Then goeth he, and taketh with himself seven other spirits more wicked than himself, and they enter in and dwell there: and the last state of that man is worse than the first. Even so shall it be also unto this wicked generation.

Years ago, I received a revelation from the Lord about this Scripture, because every time I read it, I wondered why, when the person was "swept" or "clean," would the demon enter with seven more. It is scary, isn't it? I was interpreting it the same way that most people do. One day, the Lord said, "I was talking about a hotel room."

Now, don't tell me that hotels did not exist then. Back in those times (and before those times), there was a lot of commerce and traveling. The hotel industry had already started. Since people traveled by means of camels, horses and other animals, sometimes even carrying animals for sale, the hotels had stables instead of parking garages. The animals would be cared for at the stables. Because people traveled in caravans, there were hotels big enough to take a caravan. A hotel of this kind was called a caravansary.

Luke 2:4-7
And Joseph also went up from Galilee, out of the city of Nazareth, into Judaea, unto the city of David, which is called Bethlehem; (because he was of the house and lineage of David:) To be taxed with Mary his espoused wife, being great with child. And so it was, that, while they were there, the days were accomplished that she should be delivered. And she brought forth her firstborn son, and wrapped him in swaddling clothes, and laid him in a manger; because there

was no room for them in the inn.

By that time, inns were organized to run efficiently. They had a schedule pretty much as hotels have today. They had check-in times and check-out times. They needed to know what rooms were available and what rooms were not. The time between check-out and check-in was used to sweep and garnish the empty room. Today, hotels do the same thing: they need the room vacated to clean and vacuum, and garnish it with clean linens, little bottles of shampoo, soap, and maybe even chocolates on the pillow.

So, before you can get into your room, you have to wait for check-in time, when the room is empty, swept and garnished. Then the room is ready to receive you.

When the demon is cast out, it leaves his "house" or hotel where he has been living (the body and soul of a person), and he goes to the dry places according to Scripture. But he is keeping an eye out to see if the person becomes ready again to receive him. If the person, because of his/her sins, becomes ready again, then the demon has the right to enter again and invite seven other demons. Where does he get this right? From the following Scriptures:

Leviticus 26:14-18
But if ye will not hearken unto me, and will not do all these commandments; And if ye shall despise my statutes, or if your soul abhor my judgments, so that ye will not do all my commandments, but that ye break my covenant: I also will do this unto you; I will even appoint over you terror, consumption, and the burning ague, that shall consume the eyes, and cause sorrow of heart: and ye shall sow your seed in vain, for your enemies shall eat it. And I will set my face against you, and ye shall be slain before your enemies: they

that hate you shall reign over you; and ye shall flee when none pursueth you. And if ye will not yet for all this hearken unto me, then I will punish you seven times more for your sins.

Leviticus 26:21
And if ye walk contrary unto me, and will not hearken unto me; I will bring seven times more plagues upon you according to your sins.

Leviticus 26:23-24
And if ye will not be reformed by me by these things, but will walk contrary unto me; Then will I also walk contrary unto you, and will punish you yet seven times for your sins.

Leviticus 26:27-28
And if ye will not for all this hearken unto me, but walk contrary unto me; Then I will walk contrary unto you also in fury; and I, even I, will chastise you seven times for your sins.

There are several places where the demons could go, and I believe that it is up to the Lord to say where they must go. I don't have to make that decision. In my preliminary deliverance and protection prayers, I ask the Lord for angels to come and take the demons where He wants them to go.

Demons could go to dry places, Tartarus, the Abyss or the pit, etc. I do not know. But I like to believe that when I cast out demons, they go under Jesus' feet:

Psalms 110:1
The Lord said unto my Lord, Sit thou at my right hand, until I make thine enemies thy footstool.

Matthew 22:42-45
Saying, What think ye of Christ? whose son is he? They say unto him, The Son of David. He saith unto them, How then doth David in spirit call him Lord, saying, The Lord said unto my Lord, Sit thou on my right hand, till I make thine enemies thy footstool? If David then call him Lord, how is he his son?

Mark 12:35-37
And Jesus answered and said, while he taught in the temple, How say the scribes that Christ is the Son of David? For David himself said by the Holy Ghost, The Lord said to my Lord, Sit thou on my right hand, till I make thine enemies thy footstool. David therefore himself calleth him Lord; and whence is he then his son? And the common people heard him gladly.

Luke 20:41-44
And he said unto them, How say they that Christ is David's son? And David himself saith in the book of Psalms, The Lord said unto my Lord, Sit thou on my right hand, Till I make thine enemies thy footstool. David therefore calleth him Lord, how is he then his son?

Acts 2:32-35
This Jesus hath God raised up, whereof we all are witnesses. Therefore being by the right hand of God exalted, and having received of the Father the Promise of the Holy Ghost, he hath shed forth this, which ye now see and hear. For David is not ascended into the heavens: but he saith himself, The Lord said unto my Lord, Sit thou on my right hand, Until I make thy foes thy footstool.

Hebrews 1:13
But to which of the angels said he at any time, Sit on my right hand, until I make thine enemies thy footstool?

Hebrews 10:12-13

But this man, after he had offered one sacrifice for sins for ever, sat down on the right hand of God;
From henceforth expecting till his enemies be made his footstool.

1 Corinthians 15:24-26

Then cometh the end, when he shall have delivered up the kingdom to God, even the Father; when he shall have put down all rule and all authority and power. For he must reign, till he hath put all enemies under his feet. The last enemy that shall be destroyed is death.

Hebrews 2:6-8

But one in a certain place testified, saying, What is man, that thou art mindful of him? or the son of man, that thou visitest him? Thou madest him a little lower than the angels; thou crownedst him with glory and honour, and didst set him over the works of thy hands: Thou hast put all things in subjection under his feet. For in that he put all in subjection under him, he left nothing that is not put under him. But now we see not yet all things put under him.

I believe when a Scripture is repeated a number of times in the Bible, it is because the Scripture is important. All of the above say that Jesus was told by God the Father to sit at His right hand until He makes Jesus' enemies His (Jesus') footstool. Hebrews 10:12-13 says that Jesus is expecting until his enemies are made his footstool. Hebrews 2:6-8 says not all things are put under Him yet. I believe those "things" are the demons. And I believe that when we obey and cast out demons, those demons go under Jesus' feet. This is what He is expecting, and He is sitting at the right hand of the Father waiting for all his enemies to be made His footstool.

And when will His enemies become His footstool? When all the Christians obey and cast out all the demons!

The Ministry Kit

There are several things that are handy to have around when you minister deliverance. I have put them in a briefcase so I do not forget any of them. This is what I have:

- Bible
- The Scriptures that the demons hate
- Small bottle of olive oil
- Head coverings
- Hair clips and rubber bands to keep hair away from the face
- The prayers
- Lists of names of demons (see next chapter)
- A thesaurus (see next chapter)
- Notebook
- Pens

You will also need:

- A box of facial tissues
- Paper towels
- Plastic waste baskets, buckets or small garbage cans
- Small garbage liners (grocery plastic bags can be used)
- This deliverance manual.

15

The Spirits of God

The first time I had deliverance, I felt as if I had had surgery. I felt as if something had been taken out of me violently. That feeling lasted for a day. Some people claim that they feel an emptiness inside. The evil spirits occupy a spiritual space in our soul (and body), and when they leave, some people can feel that emptiness. This emptiness can be filled only by spirits.

To finish a deliverance session, deliverance ministers bind and gag remaining demons and ask the Lord to command the angels to put those demons in boxes or cages and read them Scriptures night and day. Then they ask the Lord to fill the empty spaces in the person who received deliverance with the Spirits of God.

When I teach about this topic, my students are astounded because they have never heard about the Spirits of God. Most Christians have heard only about the Holy Spirit, but not about other Spirits of God.

1 John 4:1
Beloved, believe not every spirit, but try the spirits whether they are of God: because many false prophets are gone out into the world.

John says we should check the spirits to see if they are from God or not.

If we have cast out a spirit of hate, for instance, we should fill the space with a Spirit of Love; if we have cast out a spirit of death, we should fill the space with a Spirit of Life. The following are Spirits of God mentioned in the Scriptures. Some translations may list them differently. I believe that for every evil spirit, there is an opposite Spirit of God.

Exodus 28:3
And thou shalt speak unto all that are wise hearted, whom I have filled with the spirit of wisdom, that they may make Aaron's garments to consecrate him, that he may minister unto me in the priest's office.

Deuteronomy 34:9
And Joshua the son of Nun was full of the spirit of wisdom; for Moses had laid his hands upon him: and the children of Israel hearkened unto him, and did as the Lord commanded Moses.

Nehemiah 9:20
Thou gavest also thy good spirit to instruct them, and withheldest not thy manna from their mouth, and gavest them water for their thirst.

Job 20:3
I have heard the check of my reproach, and the spirit of my understanding causeth me to answer.

Psalms 51:10
Create in me a clean heart, O God; and renew a right spirit within me.

Proverbs 11:13
A talebearer revealeth secrets: but he that is of a faithful spirit concealeth the matter.

Proverbs 16:19
Better it is to be of an humble spirit with the lowly, than to divide the spoil with the proud.

Proverbs 17:27
He that hath knowledge spareth his words: and a man of understanding is of an excellent spirit.

Ecclesiastes 7:8
Better is the end of a thing than the beginning thereof: and the patient in spirit is better than the proud in spirit.

Isaiah 4:4
When the Lord shall have washed away the filth of the daughters of Zion, and shall have purged the blood of Jerusalem from the midst thereof by the spirit of judgment, and by the spirit of burning.

Isaiah 11:2
And the spirit of the Lord shall rest upon him, the spirit of wisdom and understanding, the spirit of counsel and might, the spirit of knowledge and of the fear of the Lord;

Isaiah 28:6
And for a spirit of judgment to him that sitteth in judgment, and for strength to them that turn the battle to the gate.

Isaiah 57:15

For thus saith the high and lofty One that inhabiteth eternity, whose name is Holy; I dwell in the high and holy place, with him also that is of a contrite and humble spirit, to revive the spirit of the humble, and to revive the heart of the contrite ones.

Daniel 6:3

Then this Daniel was preferred above the presidents and princes, because an excellent spirit was in him; and the king thought to set him over the whole realm.

Zechariah 12:10

And I will pour upon the house of David, and upon the inhabitants of Jerusalem, the spirit of grace and of supplications: and they shall look upon me whom they have pierced, and they shall mourn for him, as one mourneth for his only son, and shall be in bitterness for him, as one that is in bitterness for his firstborn.

Romans 1:4

And declared to be the Son of God with power, according to the spirit of holiness, by the resurrection from the dead:

Romans 8:15

For ye have not received the spirit of bondage again to fear; but ye have received the Spirit of adoption, whereby we cry, Abba, Father.

2 Corinthians 4:13

We having the same spirit of faith, according as it is written, I believed, and therefore have I spoken; we also believe, and therefore speak;

Galatians 6:1

Brethren, if a man be overtaken in a fault, ye which are

spiritual, restore such an one in the spirit of meekness; considering thyself, lest thou also be tempted.

Ephesians 1:17

That the God of our Lord Jesus Christ, the Father of glory, may give unto you the spirit of wisdom and revelation in the knowledge of him:

2 Timothy 1:7

For God hath not given us the spirit of fear; but of power, and of love, and of a sound mind.

Hebrews 10:29

Of how much sorer punishment, suppose ye, shall he be thought worthy, who hath trodden under foot the Son of God, and hath counted the blood of the covenant, wherewith he was sanctified, an unholy thing, and hath done despite unto the Spirit of grace?

1 Peter 4:14

If ye be reproached for the name of Christ, happy are ye; for the spirit of glory and of God resteth upon you: on their part he is evil spoken of, but on your part he is glorified.

1 John 4:6

We are of God: he that knoweth God heareth us; he that is not of God heareth not us. Hereby know we the spirit of truth, and the spirit of error.

Revelation 19:10

And I fell at his feet to worship him. And he said unto me, See thou do it not: I am thy fellowservant, and of thy brethren that have the testimony of Jesus: worship God: for the testimony of Jesus is the spirit of prophecy.

16

Names of Demons

Demons have names, but they do not necessarily keep the same names through the centuries. Some names are very old and some are up-to-date. This shows that in some cases they modernize their name. For instance, when I went to Hegewisch Church for a workshop in 1980, I heard plenty of demons giving their names as "Darth Vader". Darth Vader was an evil character in the movie *Star Wars* released in 1977. Those demons that were giving Darth Vader as their name were not "born" when the movie came out. They existed even at the time of the Garden of Eden. Before Darth Vader they had another name, and only God knows how many names they have had.

Another example is Jezebel. The demon called Jezebel now did not have that name before Queen Jezebel existed. Because Queen Jezebel acted under the influence of demons, obeyed Satan rather than God, had the prophets of God killed, got the prophets of Baal to eat at her table and did all this right in the Promised Land, the demons were delighted with her. Satan honored her by changing the name of some demons to Jezebel.

Working in casting out Jezebel demons, I found a demon called Josephine, named after the French empress Josephine, the wife of Napoleon. This is another example of a name change.

Some demons have historical names; some have very strange, old names; some have up-to-date names; and some are named only after their function, such as envy, pain, hate, etc. To know some really strange names of demons, get booklet #28, *Proper Names of Demons*, published by WRW Publications.

It is Not Necessary to Know the Name

It is not necessary to know the name of a demon to cast it out. If you know what a demon is doing to the person, you can cast it out. For instance, if a person named Mary comes to you and says, "Something is making me count backwards; I think it is a demon," you can say, "Demon that is making Mary count backwards, come out of Mary in the name of Jesus," and the demon will come out. The demon might make you work at it, but it will be cast out.

"You Can't Make Me"

A few years ago a young lady was attending my deliverance classes. She had several children, and at the time she was trying to potty-train the youngest one. She was having problems with this and was getting tired of changing diapers. One day, she sat the child on the toilet and told him to go. The child was not trying, and she was getting desperate. She received an assurance from the Holy Spirit that it was a demon in the child that was making him behave this way. As she insisted that he "go potty", the little boy would say, "You can't make me." This happened two or three times. She was wondering what the name of the demon was, and the Holy Spirit told her, "That's it! That's the name! You can't make me!" Immediately, she commanded "You can't make me" out of her child in the name of Jesus, and it came out. The child was potty-trained that day.

Proper Names of Real People

When a demon gives the proper name of a person as his own name, it means that the person with that name put a curse on the person to whom you are ministering. Many times the person to whom you are ministering will be surprised to hear the name, because he knows the person and had no idea that person was placing spells or hexes on him.

Basic Names of Demons

I use the term "basic names" to refer to the names of demons that are more common. The book, *Pigs in the Parlor,* by Frank Hammond (Impact Christian Books) has a very complete list of basic names of demons. In the book they are placed in groups of demons that work together.

I use this list of names when I start ministering. The list is helpful to jump-start a deliverance session. Sometimes when things go flat and the Holy Spirit does not tell you anything, call out the names on this list and you might have results.

The Thesaurus

A thesaurus is a dictionary of synonyms, and it is a great help to find the basic names of demons that may work together in a cluster. When you cast out a demon, look up the name of that demon in the thesaurus, and you will see the names of the demons in his group.

Names of Religious Spirits

Christians have religious demons. Some denominations may have their own religious demons according to their teachings. Catholics have many religious demons also for obvious reasons, like praying to "The Virgin". Graduates from seminaries and Bible colleges may have picked up religious demons there. All of us should get deliverance from religious demons. Some names of religious demons are: ritualism, formalism, legalism, religiosity, false gifts such as false tongues, false prophecy, etc.

My daughter, who went to an Episcopalian parochial school, had to repeat prayers over and over for years as part of her daily worship at this school. She has been delivered of many religious spirits, and she suspects that demons obtain a legal right to enter when you mindlessly repeat prayers (as Jesus told us **not** to do) such as the Scriptures known as "The Lord's Prayer."

Matthew 6:7
But when you pray, use not vain repetitions, as the heathen do: for the think that they shall be heard for their much speaking.

Jezebel

All women have the Jezebel demon to a degree. I have often encountered this demon since I started ministering. This is a tough demon to cast out, and she has a hierarchy of demons under her. I have written a book on how to cast her out called *Jezebel and the Goddesses,* published by

Impact Christian Books. It has most of the names of the demons that work with her and need to be cast out before Jezebel will come out.

Lucifer

Lucifer is a very strong demon (probably a principality) that likes to work with Jezebel, and Lucifer might also be present where there has been witchcraft. Some minor demons will give their name as Lucifer, but they are not Lucifer.

Leviathan

There is much said in the Bible about Leviathan. Job 33:34 says that he is king over all the children of pride, but I have seen more pride associated with Jezebel than with Leviathan. Symptoms of Leviathan are sleepiness, drowsiness, laziness, forgetfulness and interference with reading the Bible. Jezebel, Lucifer and Leviathan are strong demons who like to work together helping each other. When dealing with one of them, you need to isolate it from the other two with the blood of Jesus.

Incubus and Succubus

Incubus is a "male" demon that molests women at night when they sleep. The woman cannot wake up while this is happening. Some women are ashamed to report this to the deliverance minister. Succubus is the counterpart of Incubus, a "female" demon that molests men while they sleep. I find this demon often while ministering.

Lilith

At Lake Hamilton Bible Camp, it was discovered that

the demon Lilith was causing crib death. LHBC published all the details in its newsletter. Later, I was watching a TV talk show where the invited guests were mothers of children who "saw things". Most of the children were actually seeing demons. Cristina, the hostess of the show, talked to one mother who explained that her little girl, when in bed, would see a woman enter her room who would ask the girl to go with her. The little girl told her that the woman's name was Lilith.

The Cristina show is not a religious show. The people in the show did not know anything about deliverance. The little girl reported to her mother what "the woman" told her. This confirms the findings at Lake Hamilton Bible Camp.

Pastoral Madness

Because so many pastors, evangelists and other leaders believe that Christians cannot have demons, they are particularly the target of a demon called Pastoral Madness. I found out about this demon soon after I started working in the deliverance ministry.

When I started in the ministry, I could not stay in the church I had been attending, because the pastor did not want me there. I wanted to return to my first church, but the Lord impressed me to visit another church. I did not like this church, so I made an appointment with the pastor of the first church to explain to him my ministry before re-joining that church. After I had the appointment scheduled, the Lord pressured me to call the pastor of the other church, which I did. I told him that I believed the Lord wanted me to tell him about my deliverance ministry. He said he wanted me to come to his house and tell both him and his wife about it. We made the appointment for the day after the other appointment.

I met with the pastor of the first church. At first, he wanted me back in the church. I explained to him about the deliverance I had received and about the ministry I now had. He said he wanted me back in the church, but forbade me from telling anyone that I had had deliverance and from laying hands on or praying for anyone in the church. Then I asked him, "What if I am ministering somewhere and I am asked what church I attend?" The pastor decided that I had better not re-join his church.

The next day, I met with the other pastor. I told them about the deliverance ministry, and the pastor said, "My church really needs this, but if you want to teach about deliverance here, you have to become a member of this church."

It was pretty obvious to me that the Lord wanted me in this church. I agreed and became a member. Later, I asked again about teaching, and he told me the church was not ready for it yet. He asked me to teach the adult Bible class instead.

Pretty soon, I started noticing things that were not right. I wanted to leave, but the Lord would not let me. There was immorality in the church. I called the Pastor about it and his answer was, "What do you want me to do about it?" Later, I started seeing the face of the pastor before me. Any time I would quiet down, his face would appear in my mind. I was upset about it, and I called a friend to minister deliverance to me.

During the ministry, a demon manifested that would not give his name. Under my friend's questioning, the demon said he had entered through my pastor. My friend asked, "Who is your boss?" The demon answered "Pastoral Madness."

I speak with an accent. When I heard myself saying that name, it was pronounced differently than I would have pronounced it. I was delivered from the demon, and we found out that the demon came from the pastor, who had a demon called Pastoral Madness. I told the Lord I wanted to leave the church, and He said, "Now you can."

What Does Pastoral Madness Do?

During the following days, the Holy Spirit brought to my mind the work that this demon does. Have you ever wondered why pastors and TV evangelists go bad? Have you ever noticed that it is more or less the same thing happening to all of them? It has to do with money and sex. Greed and lust. Or perhaps it boils down to lust only. Lust for money, lust for fame, lust for admiration, lust for sex, lust for being considered important. Mammon. Can't get enough of it.

The Holy Spirit told me that this demon says to the pastors, "You are wonderful. You are great. God is really happy with you. You are the apple of His eye. He is so happy with you, that you could just fib a little, and He would not mind. You are special. You can do things other people cannot do. You can get away with this because God is so proud of you. You deserve more money. You deserve that Jaguar. You should not be driving anything less than the best, since you are a child of God. Get that Rolex, you deserve it. God wants you to have it, because He is so happy with you. You need to extract more money from the congregation, so you can pay yourself a higher salary. You need a larger house; the one you are living in is not the kind of house God wants for you. Get some guards to protect you;

don't let ordinary people touch you. You are special, you are anointed. You don't have time for their problems. Your wife is not the woman that God wanted you to marry. She is not a help meet for you. The woman that God has for you is (the evangelist, the singer, the secretary, the prophetess, etc.). You need a bigger building. Buy a big tract of land, you need to build the biggest church in town, that's what God wants. You need a helicopter...you need a private jet," etc.

The demon starts perverting the pastor little by little. The pastor fails in little things first, then in bigger things, until there is a scandal that is published by the press. We have seen this happen nationally and locally.

I remember visiting a church where the three center front rows were perennially reserved for a group of mature ladies who idolized the pastor. The pastor seemed to be very pleased with it. A few years later, a scandal hit the local newspapers: the pastor had been stealing money from the church and having an affair with the secretary.

You may recall a pastor who had a big ministry, a Bible school and a chain of radio stations, repenting on TV of his immorality, with tears rolling down his face, only to do the same thing again not much later. Even the national news magazines displayed this scandal on the covers.

There is a lot of forgiving and restoring when these things happen, but there is never casting out of demons. If the demons would have been cast out before these men had even become pastors or evangelists, all the corruption might have been averted. But these pastors and evangelists are the ones who come against the ministry of deliverance, saying that Christians do not have demons.

The Dust Demons

A friend called me to minister to a friend of hers. This woman told me she could not clean her house. Her house was cluttered, and she could not bring herself to throw anything away. When she purposed in her mind to tackle some cleaning, she would feel weak and would have to lay down. She just could not get around to cleaning her house. The demons cast out of her worked as a team. The main demon, in her case, was the Prince of Dust. He called himself Dust. The ones working under Dust were: dirt, clutter, keeping things, old things, disorganization, trash, weakness and pain.

Names of Diseases

Diseases sometimes are completely demonic, or partly demonic. Years ago, I was getting ready to go to Mexico where I was going to conduct a mass deliverance in a church. The Lord told me to make a list of names of diseases and call them out at the end of the other list that I had. There was tremendous deliverance with the names of diseases, and the Pastor's mother in law was healed of Diabetes.

Names of Diseases

Heart:
Palpitations, Arrhythmia, Heart Attack, Thrombosis, Coronary, Embolism, Paralysis, Pectoral Angina, Tachycardia, Apoplexy, Pericarditis, Cardiomyopathy, Valvepathy, Congenital Abnormality.

Blood and Veins:
Hypertension, Hypotension, Anemia, Leukemia, Clots, Thrombosis, Hemophilia, Arteriosclerosis, Aneurism, Lymphoma, Trombocitophenia.

Liver:
Neoplasia, Cirrhosis, Acute Hepatitis, Hepatitis B, Chronic Hepatitis, Cancer.

Gall Bladder:
Calculus, Inflammation, Colecistitis.

Pancreas:
Diabetes, Pancreatitis, Cancer.

Brain:
Tumors, Epilepsy, Parkinson's Disease, Alzheimer's Disease, Senility, Aneurysm, Addictions, Dementia, Insomnia, Sleep Disturbances.

Nerves:
Multiple Sclerosis, Herpes, Neuritis, Neuralgia, Sciatica.

Thyroid:
Hypothyroidism, Hyperthyroidism, Thyroiditis, Gout, Hashimoto's Disease, Grave's Disease.

Lungs and Breathing:
Asthma, Sinusitis, Allergies, Pneumonia, Emphysema, Influenza, Flu, Grippe, Colds, Bronchitis,
Tuberculosis, TB, Sarcoidosis, Cystic Fibrosis, Cancer, Apnea, Snoring.

Mouth, Trachea, Larynx, Esophagus and Stomach:
Tooth Decay, Cavities, Gum Disease, Ulcers, Hiatal Hernia, Gastritis, Digestive Problems, Cancer.

Kidneys, Bladder and Urethra:
Glomerulonephritis, Renal Failure, Tubular Necrosis,

Chronic renal Insufficiency, Cystitis, Lithiasis, Stones, Neoplasia, Tumor, Cancer.

Intestines, Colon and Rectum:
Colitis, Polyps, Gas, Cancer, Irritable Colon, Diarrhea, Malabsorption Syndrome, Crohn's Disease,
Achalasia, Diverticulitis.

Eyes:
Glaucoma, Myopia, Astigmatism, Estrabism, Cataracts, Conjunctivitis, Blindness, Infections, Floaters, Dryness.

Ears:
Deafness, Titinus, Deaf-Mute, Vertigo, Dizziness, Infection.

Bones, Joints and Ligaments:
Arthritis, Osteoporosis, Paget's Disease, Osteomalacia, Cancer.

Muscles:
Muscular Dystrophy, Myasthenia Gravis, Lou Gehrig's Disease, Multiple Sclerosis, Lupus, Scleroderma.

Skin:
Warts, Tags, Acne, Psoriasis, Herpes, Eczema, Fungus, Melanomas, Cancer.

Reproductive Organs:
Irregular Menstruation, Painful Menstruation, Curses of Infertility, Hanna's Curse, Painful Delivery, Eve's Curse (*Genesis 3*), Early Menopause, Breast Cancer, Hirsutism, Hormonal Upsets, Impotency, Galactorrhea, Ovaric Cysts.

Metabolism:
Gout, Obesity, Anorexia, Hypercholesterolemia (High Cholesterol), Galactosemia, Marfan's Syndrome, Amino Acid's Disturbances.

Cancer:
Melanoma, Lymphoma, Carcinoma, Stomach Cancer, Uterine Cancer, Ovaric Cancer, Breast Cancer, Skin Cancer, Lung Cancer, Liver Cancer, Pancreatic Cancer, Esophagus Cancer, Mouth Cancer, tongue Cancer, Lip Cancer, Kidney Cancer, Bladder Cancer, Prostate Cancer, Brain Cancer, Bone Cancer, Lymph Nodule Cancer.

Miscellaneous:
Germs, Bacteria, Protozoa, Viruses, Parasites, Fungi, Yeasts, Spirit of Infirmity, Spirit of Death, Spirit of Coma, Spirit of Paralysis, Vegetal, Traumas.

Obesity Demons

Once, when I was ministering to a woman who wanted demons of obesity cast out, demons came out stating their names, and I took notes. The list follows.

Obesity Demons
Obesity, Overweight, Fat
Plump, Pleasantly Plump

Cravings, Craving fat, Craving food
Craving fried food, Craving sweets
Sweet tooth, Craving chocolate
Craving rich desserts

Over-eating, Second helpings

Desire to pile food up in the plate
Old hunger, Surfeiting
Storing fat
Demons storing fat
Demons holding back the stored fat
Demons preventing the stored fat from going to be burned
Demons putting off the burning of the fat

Laziness, Weakness, Lack of will
Too tired to exercise

Hungry, Desire to eat

Low metabolism
Demons lowering the metabolism
Demons in the glands that have to do with the metabolism

Frustration, Unhappiness, Anxiety
Anxiety provoked by demons to make one eat.

(Break the curse of obesity)
(Break the curse of Eli)

Cellulite
(Break the curse of cellulite)

Demons who store fat under the skin

Demons who work to get the body's biochemistry out of balance

Demons impairing fat metabolism

Demons producing excess insulin

Demons interfering with the body's thermogenics

Take authority over the thyroid and command it to start thermogenesis

(Break curses and demons who entered with crash diets and other diets by name of diets:Weight Watchers, Atkins, Cabbage Soup, etc.)

Take authority and command it to turn off the excessive fat storing mechanism and turn on the fat-burning mechanism.

17

Scriptures That The Demons Hate

In my experience, reading these Scriptures to stubborn demons have made them come out. They do not want to hear these Scriptures. I do not just read them, I make comments to the demons also, reinforcing what these Scriptures say.

Matthew 16:18-19
And I say also unto thee, That thou art Peter, and upon this rock I will build my church; and the gates of hell shall not prevail against it. And I will give unto thee the keys of the kingdom of heaven: and whatsoever thou shalt bind on earth shall be bound in heaven: and whatsoever thou shalt loose on earth shall be loosed in heaven.

Luke 10:19
Behold, I give unto you power to tread on serpents and scorpions, and over all the power of the enemy: and nothing shall by any means hurt you.

Ephesians 1:19-23

And what is the exceeding greatness of his power to us-ward who believe, according to the working of his mighty power, Which he wrought in Christ, when he raised him from the dead, and set him at his own right hand in the heavenly places, Far above all principality, and power, and might, and dominion, and every name that is named, not only in this world, but also in that which is to come: And hath put all things under his feet, and gave him to be the head over all things to the church, Which is his body, the fulness of him that filleth all in all.

Ephesians 3:10-11

To the intent that now unto the principalities and powers in heavenly places might be known by the church the manifold wisdom of God, According to the eternal purpose which he purposed in Christ Jesus our Lord:

Ephesians 3:20-21

Now unto him that is able to do exceeding abundantly above all that we ask or think, according to the power that worketh in us, Unto him be glory in the church by Christ Jesus throughout all ages, world without end. Amen.

2 Corinthians 10:3-4

For though we walk in the flesh, we do not war after the flesh: (For the weapons of our warfare are not carnal, but mighty through God to the pulling down of strong holds;)

Colossians 1:12-17

Giving thanks unto the Father, which hath made us meet to be partakers of the inheritance of the saints in light: Who hath delivered us from the power of darkness, and hath translated us into the kingdom of his dear Son: In whom we have redemption through his blood, even the forgiveness of

sins: Who is the image of the invisible God, the firstborn of every creature: For by him were all things created, that are in heaven, and that are in earth, visible and invisible, whether they be thrones, or dominions, or principalities, or powers: all things were created by him, and for him:
And he is before all things, and by him all things consist.

Colossians 2:9-10
For in him dwelleth all the fulness of the Godhead bodily. And ye are complete in him, which is the head of all principality and power:

Colossians 2:14-15
Blotting out the handwriting of ordinances that was against us, which was contrary to us, and took it out of the way, nailing it to his cross; And having spoiled principalities and powers, he made a shew of them openly, triumphing over them in it.

Revelation 1:18
I am he that liveth, and was dead; and, behold, I am alive for evermore, Amen; and have the keys of hell and of death.

There may be other very effective Scriptures to cast out demons, but these are my favorites.

18

Prayers

I obtained the following prayers for protection and the basic prayers to destroy legal rights at Hegewisch Baptist Church during a deliverance workshop in the summer of 1980. They are very effective, and Pastor Worley would not minister to anyone who, as he used to say, "had not taken the prayers," first.

When To Use The Prayers

The prayer of protection should be said by the minister every time that the minister is going to minister deliverance to a person. The basic prayers are said by the person the first time the person receives deliverance. It is not necessary for the person to repeat them after the first session; however, it is not a bad idea to pray them once in a while. While my daughter was editing and proofreading my book, she was reading out loud and began to have deliverance when she got to the prayers chapter!

How To Use The Basic Prayers

The minister reads a portion of the prayer, and the person repeats after the minister. Repeating what the minister says makes the person concentrate on the prayers. I have discovered that some people cannot remember but a few words, while others can repeat a whole sentence. When the person has trouble remembering, it may be a demon interfering. You could bind it. If that does not work, make note of it for specific deliverance of lack of retention, or memory, or forgetfulness.

For better results, the person should repeat with meaning and understanding of what he is saying.

Some people will attempt to grab the prayers out of your hands and read them themselves, which indicates spirits of rebellion and unsubmissiveness.

Depending on the prayer, you will have to stop and give the person time to do what the prayer indicates. I sometimes step away to give them privacy depending on the circumstances.

During your initial conversation with the person, you may have formed a list of the occult practices with which the person was involved. When you get to the "Confession of the Occult" prayer, your notes will help the person confess and repent of those specific things. If you don't have the person's list, go over the list of occult practices, take notes and then say the prayer.

Welcome This Interruption

Many times, the person starts having deliverance in the middle of saying the prayers. Because it is the work of the Holy Spirit, follow suit and cast out the demons, then continue with the prayers.

You might want to copy and laminate the following prayers to have them handy when you minister.

Prayer for Protection

Father, in the name of Jesus we come before you. We thank You that your Word says that You have given us power to tread on serpents and scorpions and all the power of the enemy, and nothing shall by any means hurt us. Lord, we are gathered together in your name to obey Your Word and cast demons out. Father, we ask You that You send Your angels to completely surround us in all directions to cut off any help that might come from the powers of the air to the demons that we are going to cast out. We also ask for angels to come and take the demons that we cast out to the place You want them to go. And, Lord, also send angels to our homes, to our (husband, wife), to our children, to our children's homes and protect their children, pets and possessions. Protect our dear ones wherever they are and whatever they are doing, as we obey You in casting demons out. In the name of Jesus, amen.

Basic Prayers to Destroy Legal Rights of Demons

Warfare Prayer: Heavenly Father, I bow in worship and praise before You. I cover myself with the blood of the Lord Jesus Christ as my protection. I surrender myself completely and unreservedly in every area of my life to You. I take a stand against all the workings of Satan that would hinder me in my prayer life. I address myself only to the true and Living God and refuse any involvement of Satan in my prayer. Satan, I command you in the name of the Lord Jesus Christ to leave my presence with all of your demons. I bring the blood of the Lord Jesus Christ between us. I resist all the endeavors of Satan and his wicked spirits to rob me of the will of God. I choose to be transformed by the renewing of my mind. I pull down the stronghold of Satan.

General Confession: Lord Jesus Christ, I believe that You are the Son of God, that You are the Messiah come in the flesh to destroy the works of the devil. You died on the cross for my sins and rose again from the dead the third day. I now confess my sins and repent. (Stop-do this now). I ask You to forgive me and cleanse me now from all sin. Thank You for redeeming me, cleansing me and sanctifying me in Your blood.

Forgiveness Prayer: Lord, I have a confession to make. I have not loved but resented certain people and have unforgiveness in my heart. I call upon You, Lord, to help me forgive them. I do now forgive (say who, living or dead). I ask You to forgive them also, Lord. I now forgive and accept myself in the name of Jesus Christ.

Prayer to Break Soul Ties: Father, I break and renounce evil soul ties that I have or may have had with (lodges, gangs, adulterers, family members, friends, cults, promises, etc.). I renounce these evil soul ties, break them and wash them away with the shed blood of the Lord Jesus Christ.

Prayer to Loose From Domination: In the name of Jesus Christ, I now renounce, break and loose myself from all demonic subjection to my parents, grandparents (name all suspects) and any other human beings, dead or alive, who have dominated me in any way. I thank You, Lord, for setting me free.

Loosing From Witchcraft Works: In the name of Jesus Christ, I now renounce, break and loose myself and my children from all evil curses, charms, hexes, vexes, spells, jinxes, psychic powers, bewitchment, witchcraft and sorcery that has been put upon me or my family line from any persons or from any occult or psychic sources, and I cancel all connected or related demons, and I command them to leave me. I thank You, Lord, for setting me free.

Confession of Pride: Father, I come to you in the name of Jesus Christ. I know that pride is an abomination to You, that a haughty look, a lying tongue, hands that shed innocent blood, feet that are swift in running to mischief, a false witness that speaks lies, and he that sows discord among brethren are an abomination to You. Father, I renounce all these things and turn away from them. I humble myself before You and come to You as a little child.

"Coming to Jesus" Deliverance Prayer: I come to You, Jesus, as my Deliverer. You know all my needs (tell Him now). You know all the things that bind, torment, defile and harass me. I now loose myself from every dark spirit, from every evil influence, from every satanic bondage, from every spirit in me that is not the Spirit of the Lord, and I command all such spirits to leave me now in the name of the Lord Jesus Christ. I now confess that my body is the temple of the Holy Spirit, redeemed, cleansed sanctified by the blood of the Lord Jesus Christ. Therefore, Satan has no place in me, no power over me, through the blood of Jesus Christ.

Derek Prince's "Blood of Jesus" Prayer: Through the blood of Jesus, I am redeemed from the hand of the devil. Through the blood of Jesus, all my sins are forgiven. The blood of Jesus Christ, God's Son, cleanses me continually from all sin. Through the blood of Jesus, I am justified, made holy, set apart to God. My body is a temple for the Holy Spirit, redeemed, cleansed, sanctified by the blood of Jesus. Therefore, Satan has no part in me, no power over me, by the blood of the Lord Jesus Christ. I renounce Satan, I loose myself from him, I command him to leave me in the name of the Lord Jesus Christ.

Prayer for the Confession of Involvement in the Occult: Lord, I now confess seeking from Satan the help that should only come from You. I now confess as sin (name all of it) and also those that I cannot remember. Lord, I now repent and renounce these sins and ask You to forgive me. I rebuke Satan, I count all things of Satan as my enemies. In the name of Jesus Christ, I now close the door to all occult practices, and I command all the occult spirits to leave me in the name of Jesus Christ.

Confession of Unbelief and Doubt: Father, I confess my unbelief and doubt as sin, and I ask You to forgive me for them.

Prayer for Deliverance of Mind Control: In the name of Jesus Christ, I command Satan and all his demons to loose my mind. I ask You, Father, to send angels to break, cut and sever all ties, bands, fetters and bonds in my mind, whether they exist by word or deed. I now ask the Lord to send the Spirits of the Lord, the Fear of the Lord, Counsel, Might, Wisdom, Knowledge, and Understanding into me and my family.

Dr. Marcus Haggard's Prayer to Restore the Soul: Father, I come to You in the name of Jesus Christ, and I ask You to send angels to gather the pieces of my soul and restore them to their rightful place in me. With the full power and authority of the Lord Jesus Christ, I ask for You to send Your angels to unearth and break all vessels where the fragments of my soul are, all bonds and bindings that have been put upon my soul, willingly or unaware. I ask You to have them free my soul from all bondage by whatever means are required, and I agree and say, Father, that the power of the Lord Jesus Christ is effective to do this. Now, Father, I ask You to send Your angels to gather and restore all the pieces of my fragmented mind, will and emotions, and bring them into proper and original position perfectly, as You planned them when You created Adam and Eve in the Garden of Eden. In the authority of Jesus Christ, I break and cast out, and return to the sender, the power of all curses upon my head and upon my soul.

End of Basic Prayers.

Hegewisch Baptist Church Prayer

In the name of Jesus Christ, my Lord and Savior, I bind all principalities, powers of the air, wickedness in high places, powers, thrones, dominions, world rulers and strong men over (name). I bind witchcraft, witchcraft control, mind-blinding spirits, spirits that block or bind the will, mind control, destruction, lust, rebellion, rejection, schizophrenia, paranoia, anger, hatred, resentment, bitterness, unforgiveness, unteachableness, deception, Ahab and Jezebel, doubt and unbelief, fears, drugs, rock and rap music, hypnosis, hypnotic trance and alcohol. I bind kings, princes and world rulers for each spirit here named. I strip each spirit and its hierarchy of power, armor and rank, and separate each one from the other.

I bind all evil touching the senses of sight, smell, taste, touch and hearing; all evil against the emotions; and all evil against the seven points of the body used by witchcraft (heel of the spine, spleen, navel, heart, throat, between the eyes and top of the head). I bind all evil in the systems of the body (reproductive, skeletal, muscular, digestive, excretory, endocrine, respiratory, nervous and circulatory).

I bind any and all evil powers giving aid or pulling these things in your body toward evil by means of energy drawn from the sun, moon, stars, planets, constellations, earth, air, wind, fire, water, light, darkness, matter and elements, and from lines and/or circles used against us.

I bind any transfer of spirits in family, friends or associates (name the people whose demons you are binding and from whom you forbid transference). I break, sever, clip and sear with the blood of Jesus any soul ties among these persons, and I place the blood of Jesus over the mind, emotions and will of each individual.

Each and every spirit named in this prayer is to be bound in (name of the person and your name). This prayer will also be in effect for every person whom (same names) meets. Spirits from the netherworld, spirits between, over and around (same names) are to be completely bound in the name of Jesus Christ.

I loose the spirits of God (*Isaiah 11:2*) and any others indicated upon (same names) along with the spirits of Mercy and Grace. I place shields over the minds of these persons to protect from infiltration of end-time Mind Control.

19

Recommended Books and Websites

Pigs in the Parlor, by Frank Hammond
Publisher: Impact Christian Books

Host of Hell series of books, by Win Worley
Publisher: WRW Publications

Jezebel And The Goddesses, by Mitsi Burton
Publisher: Impact Christian Books

Books by Bill Banks
Publisher: Impact Christian Books

IMPACT CHRISTIAN BOOKS
Impact Christian Books has many deliverance books by different authors. Write or call for a catalog or visit their website.

www.impactchristianbooks.com

332 Leffingwell Ave, Suite 101
Kirkwood, MO, USA 63122
Phone 314-822-3309

HEGEWISCH BAPTIST CHURCH
Hegewisch Baptist Church has deliverance workshops several times a year. You can buy all of the WRW Publications books and recordings at the church or through their website, plus books and recordings by other authors.

www.hbcdelivers.org

H.B.C.
8711 Cottage Grove Ave.
Highland, IN, USA 46322
Phone 219-838-9410

WRW Publications
P.O. Box 852626
Mesquite, TX, USA 75181

FRANK HAMMOND (The Children's Bread Ministry)
Frank Hammond's book, ***Pigs in the Parlor***, has been a bestseller for many years. He also has authored other books on deliverance.

www.thechildrensbread.net

P.O. Box 789
Plainview, TX, USA 79073

LAKE HAMILTON BIBLE CAMP (LHBC)
LHBC holds deliverance workshops several times a year, always on holidays. You can stay at the camp and have your

meals there, and it is very affordable. They have a large selection of books and recordings on deliverance and other Christian subjects. You can see the catalog on their website.

www.lakehamiltonbiblecamp.com

6191 Central Ave.
Hot Springs, AR, 71913-9646
P.O. Box 21516
Hot Springs, AR, USA, 71903
Phone 501-525-8204
72LBC@cablelynx.com

DEMONBUSTER.
Stan and Elizabeth Madrak's website has plenty of good teachings and information about deliverance and printable documents about different demons which can be used in ministering deliverance.

www.demonbuster.com

JESUS THE DELIVERER CHURCH
Jesus the Deliverer Church is located in Sugar Land, Texas. The church has a school of deliverance to train deliverance ministers.

www.Jesusthedeliverer.org

Pastor Mitsi Burton
P.O. Box 2854
Sugar Land, TX 77487-2854
mitsiburton@ev1.net

Finally, my brethren,
be strong in the Lord
and in the power of His might.

Ephesians 6:10